History, Disrupted

Jason Steinhauer

History, Disrupted

How Social Media and the World Wide Web Have
Changed the Past

Jason Steinhauer
Washington, DC, USA

ISBN 978-3-030-85116-3   ISBN 978-3-030-85117-0   (eBook)
https://doi.org/10.1007/978-3-030-85117-0

This Palgrave Macmillan imprint is published by the registered company Springer Nature
Switzerland AG.
The registered company address is: Gewerbestrasse 11, 6330 Cham, Switzerland

ACKNOWLEDGMENTS

This book could not have been written without two libraries, the U.S. Library of Congress and Falvey Memorial Library.

The Library of Congress is, quite simply, the most inspiring place in the world to write and do research. Sitting in the Main Reading Room of the Library's Thomas Jefferson Building is like being wrapped in a warm blanket made of wisdom while having a rich cup of enlightenment in your hands. There is nowhere on Earth quite like it. I've been fortunate to experience the Library as a staff member and as a scholar. For seven years, I worked at the Library of Congress, four-and-a-half in the Library's residential scholars center, The John W. Kluge Center. It was in those offices on the north side of the Thomas Jefferson Building that the seeds for this book were planted. The first conversations I had were with two scholars-in-residence at the Kluge Center, David Grinspoon and John Bew. Apart from advice, what I gained most from them was encouragement. They recognized I was onto something and told me to keep digging. For that, I am forever grateful. The other formative influence was my boss, Carolyn Brown—herself a brilliant scholar. Dr. Brown believed in my capacity to grow into an author. She allowed me to theorize about history's place in the world when I had only an inkling of what I was talking about. She knew that by talking it out I would uncover new questions, and for many afternoons inside her office we had long, enriching conversations. She demonstrated each day what true wisdom and grace looked like.

Once I left the Library for academia, I returned often. I was fortunate to spend semester breaks as a guest of the Kluge Center to research and write. It was at the Kluge Center that the first draft of this book was completed. I'm grateful to John Haskell, Travis Hensley, Dan Turello and Michael Stratmoen for their hospitality.

The second and third drafts of this book were researched at Falvey Memorial Library. Access to hundreds of journal articles and e-books was gained through Falvey. Special gratitude to archivist Beaudry Allen and digital scholarship librarian Erica Hayes for their guidance and patience. Their contributions made several elements of this book possible.

Since 2014 I've had numerous conversations about how history gets communicated on the Web. I've been enriched by the insights of many people, but particularly wish to acknowledge: Marla Miller, Jennifer Hart, Charisse L'Pree Corsbie-Massay, Kathryn C. Brownell, Nicole Hemmer, Rebecca Onion, Julie Golia, Cathy Stanton, Jim Grossman, Dane Kennedy, John Dichtl, Christian Ostermann, Nathaniel Comfort, Eric Olson, Glenn Hampson, Jessica Pearson, Ernesto Capello, Claire Lanier, Gregory Parker, Joshua C. Birk, Brian Rosenwald, Lindsay Sarah Krasnoff, Amanda Moniz, Paul Sturtevant, Yoni Applebaum, Ed Ayers, Stephen Robertson, Jamia Wilson, Eric Schulze, Richard Price, Vincent Brown, Lily Rothman, Carol Curiel, Shola Lynch, David Myers, Hamza Choudery, Annie Ulevitch, Pooja Sarvaiya, Javaughan Lawrence and Xiao Ling. My gratitude to the University of Massachusetts Amherst and Purdue University for their support of a "History Communication" summit in 2016.

Robin Colucci, Becky Sweren, Laura Tillman, Seven McDonald, Claire Atkin, Kent Holland, Adam Lederer and Sean Griffith offered invaluable feedback at various stages of the writing process. My editor Andy Kifer worked diligently to refine my ideas and concepts until they rang true on the page. Molly Beck and Lucy Kidwell at Palgrave Macmillan stood behind this project every step of the way. This book could also not have been written without Clubhouse. Thank you to Paul Davison, Rohan Seth, Harsh and the Pals, Testflighters and the tens of thousands of people in the History Club.

Finally, I wish to thank my gorgeous soulmate. She has changed me in so many ways that I've already lost count. I love you forever.

CONTENTS

1 Introduction   1

2 *e*-History: Not Quite History and Not Quite the Past   9

3 The Crowd-Sourced Past   19

4 Nostalgia on Demand   33

5 The Viral Past   43

6 The Visual Past   57

7 The Newsworthy Past   73

8 The Storytelling Past   87

9   History.AI   99

10   Does History Have a Future?   107

Notes   119

Index   155

CHAPTER 1

Introduction

In August 2015, Ty Seidule went viral. Wearing his U.S. Army uniform decorated with epaulets on each shoulder, the former Professor and Head of the Department of History at West Point starred in a five-minute video for PragerU about why slavery was the single most important cause of the U.S. Civil War. The video had 34.4 million views on the PragerU website, 12 million views on Facebook and 2.6 million views on YouTube.[1] It was, at the time, one of the most-viewed history videos ever recorded.[2]

Seidule's video was an example of what I call *e*-**history**, discrete media products that package an element, or elements, of the past for consumption on the social Web and which try to leverage the social Web in order to gain visibility. Examples of *e*-history include history YouTube videos, history Twitter threads, history Instagram posts, podcasts and history Wikipedia pages. Different types of *e*-history rely on different mechanisms to reach our eyes: Wikipedia entries rely on the "crowd-sourced past"; Instagram posts rely on "the visual past"; and history-themed news articles rely on the "newsworthy past." The PragerU video was an example of what I call the "viral past," a type of *e*-history that purposefully seeks to spark contagion through social networks by provoking rapid sharing within a short period of time. Achieving virality helped to grant it influence, credibility and authoritativeness, as well as advance an agenda.

For PragerU, that agenda is to counteract a purported "liberal orthodoxy" inside American universities, particularly within history departments.[3] Created by Conservative radio host Dennis Prager, PragerU is a

J. Steinhauer, *History, Disrupted*,
https://doi.org/10.1007/978-3-030-85117-0_1

multi-million-dollar media company that distributes content across the Web and on college campuses. A viral *e*-history video about the U.S. Civil War served to validate PragerU as an authoritative source, remind viewers that it was a Republican president, Abraham Lincoln, who issued the Emancipation Proclamation, and reassert American exceptionalism by arguing that it was to "America's everlasting credit" that it fought a war to abolish slavery.[4] Progressive activists, journalists and academics have criticized PragerU's videos as indoctrination and incorrect with their facts.[5] But the social Web does not privilege facts; it privileges getting noticed and signals of attention. The virality of PragerU's *e*-history video resulted, in part, from it being a cleverly crafted piece of media and, in part, from it being part of a broader political battle between Conservatives and Progressives on how to define the American past—a struggle that predates YouTube by nearly 100 years.[6]

Why does this matter? Because today there are millions of history videos, history blogs, history memes, history podcasts, history social media accounts and historically informed news articles on the Web competing for our attention, advancing political and commercial agendas, and actively re-shaping what we know about the past. Some content goes viral; others do not. Some amass millions of views; others are barely seen. Some are accurate; some are not. Some are created by professional historians and informed by scholarship; others are made by journalists, history enthusiasts, teenagers, hobbyists, white supremacists, conspiracy theorists and foreign disinformation agents. It can often be difficult to determine which *e*-history is created by whom.

The sum effect has been the creation of a vast and expansive *e*-history universe over the past two decades that it is now as large—or larger—as any category of content on the Web. The social Web plays an enormous role in shaping the histories we encounter. A 2020 study by the Frameworks Institute found that pop culture, social media and the news media are playing an increasingly larger role in how the public thinks about the past.[7] High school teachers repeatedly tell me their students form their ideas about history from what they see on social media. A college student told me that she and her peers get their history from Twitter threads, op-eds, news stories and Wikipedia and that her younger brother gets his history from 15-minute videos on YouTube.[8] Another student told me that on any given day she watches five history videos on YouTube just while making dinner.[9] A journalist told me she gets her history primarily from Instagram,[10] while a high school student in California told me she gets her history primarily from TikTok.[11] How we understand, learn and communicate history has been completely disrupted by technology, historical information now a fragmented and atomized part of the news feed, intertwined with the onslaught of information that re-shapes our perceptions of reality each day.

This proliferation of information about the past online does not equate to a better understanding of history, however. The fragmentary nature of e-history of widely varying quality and agendas, with no uniform ethics or standards, compels individuals to try and derive meaning from simplistic, controversial, pseudo-academic and conspiratorial sources intermixed with scholarly and journalistic ones. The results can be confounding. One college student told me the amount of historical information she saw online was so overwhelming that it was nearly impossible to find what was useful. Exploring the past online from hyperlink to hyperlink "sucks you in," she said, "but you don't learn anything."[12] A friend in Silicon Valley lamented there was so much history content on the Web that it was increasingly difficult to decipher what deserved serious consideration.[13] A tech policy analyst in New York confessed that even though he engaged with online history content regularly, he forgot it shortly afterward.[14] And a journalist confided that even despite the plethora of e-history available, searching and discovering historical information remained time-consuming and challenging.[15] More historical information online does not translate to greater ease in finding, learning or understanding that information. It may, in fact, have the opposite effect.[16]

This book, then, seeks to chart this vast universe of e-history in order to better understand how the social Web has changed our understanding of the past. It digs below the surface of e-history to reveal what agendas are at work, what tactics are used to achieve visibility, how the platforms dictate what pasts we encounter and which we never see, and how Web users can be better consumers of historical information online. This book argues that e-history has grown so pervasive and omnipresent that it has come to represent what we expect *all* history to be. Its values and mores—intimately shaped by the values and mores of Silicon Valley—have changed the definition of history right before our very eyes.

Returning to the Ty Seidule video, then, what caused it to become a highly visible form of e-history? Timing mattered. Less than two months earlier, a 21-year-old named Dylann Roof entered the Emanuel African Methodist Episcopal Church in Charleston, South Carolina, and murdered nine people. Photographs of Roof showed him brandishing the

Confederate flag, reigniting a debate online and offline about the flag's significance and presence in American life. Media outlets reached out to historians for their perspectives, including Seidule. His video resonated with the news cycle and ongoing political debates.

Framing also mattered. The cause of the war was framed as a question not a settled conclusion, the alleged controversy around the question foregrounded within the video's first ten seconds. A question and a controversy served as a useful hook to grab the viewer's attention. The video also presented a symbolic juxtaposition: a white U.S. Army Officer, his chest decorated with medals, speaking about the enslavement of African Americans and the war fought to end it. The video was short—slightly over five minutes long—and professionally edited, making it attractive and easily shareable. It was posted to YouTube and Facebook, leveraging those platforms' algorithms and recommendations. Finally, the producer of the video mattered; PragerU's financial resources enabled it to distribute the video across the social Web. One analysis found PragerU ranked among the ten biggest political spenders on Facebook.[17]

Seidule is not the first historian to argue that slavery caused the U.S. Civil War, an assessment shared by nearly all in the profession. How *e*-history comes to our attention, then, has little to do with the accuracy of the information. The prevailing factors that bring *e*-history content to our attention are algorithms, social networks, how the content is framed, its relevance to the news cycle, politics, commercial motivations, power dynamics, misinformation and disinformation campaigns, and our own perceptions of history and its role in society. Subject matters rise to the top of the news feed due to political agendas or commercial interests, not because of their scholarly or factual merits. The social Web privileges the *attributes* of a piece of content more than its *veracity* or *accuracy*. The social Web has evolved into a competing marketplace of symbols, predicated on the delivery of information quickly and efficiently. *e*-history has evolved along with it. The more potent *e*-history operates as a symbol, the more likely it is to appear on our screens. Much of what *e*-history does is to flatten historical understanding into a competing war of symbols, deployed on a fast-moving Web in order to win arguments about the present. *e*-history promises quick and satisfying answers to complex questions and phenomena, providing the source material from which opinions can be formed and soundbites can be created. Its "good enough" historical understanding becomes the foundation for participation in whatever online debate may be happening at the moment—regardless of whether the information comes from a professional historian, Google, Wikipedia, Twitter, Instagram, *The New York Times*, Hardcore History, Crash Course or Russia Today. *e*-history provides continual reassurances that we know enough about the past—and can learn enough history on our own—simply because we see so much of it. Its principal outcome has not been education, but rather to embed the values of the social Web deeper into our lives. The history we privilege becomes not what deciphers the complexity of the past with rigor and fidelity, but what best succeeds at best capturing our attention in a given moment.

The explosion of *e*-history has occurred simultaneously with a series of crises in the history profession. History enrollments have plummeted at four-year colleges and universities;[18] history departments and history museums face severe budget cuts;[19] and scholarly books and articles by academics are read in smaller numbers.[20] Technology has not only disrupted how we learn history; it has disrupted the entire history profession. The Web and social media have birthed new forms of communicating history that, over time, have made the classroom lecture, the scholarly monograph and the journal article feel increasingly antiquated and impenetrable as new forms of history communication better accommodate the sensibilities of digital consumers. The prevalence and popularity of *e*-history have created difficult conditions to communicate history in other ways. *e*-history is so pervasive that, for many Web users, it has superseded the need for history classes, history lectures, history books or professional historians.

For these reasons, I and others have worked for the past several years to create the subfield of History Communication, which explores the implications of history being communicated across the Web and social media and prepares historians, journalists and content creators for how to communicate historical scholarship effectively and ethically in a twenty-first-century media environment. While this book is not a *cri de coeur* for the field of History Communication, it is part of the journey of forming such a field and articulating its function. The values of Silicon Valley and Internet capitalism have affected history's place in American society in more ways than have been previously articulated. The Web and social media reward and incentivize the production of *e*-history that is best aligned with their values and mores. The Web's incentive structures have dictated patterns in *e*-history creation that are, in many ways, antithetical to professional history—at times purposefully so. As *e*-history proliferates at astonishing rates—and as we celebrate what *e*-history achieves as opposed to how well it educates—it may lead to the demise of professional history as we know it. The tail of online success may wag the dog of discerning what might have actually occurred in the past with honesty, integrity, deep research and critical thinking.

How did this happen? The first chapter of this book will explain how e-history emerged out of a clash of values between professional history and Web 2.0. Professional history is a time-consuming, intellectual endeavor that privileges expertise and is believed by its practitioners and supporters to have an intrinsic value to society. This stands in sharp contrast to how the social Web has evolved, which is largely a user-centric, data-driven, commercial enterprise predicated on scale, speed and efficiency, and that rewards extrinsic measures of valuation. The transposition of professional history into this milieu has birthed new forms of communicating history that, taken together, now comprise the dizzying universe of e-history.

The next chapters will retrace how different parts of the e-history universe came into being, while also revealing what mechanisms make some history online visible while obscuring others. All e-history wants to be seen, for being visible on the social Web is the pathway to online and offline influence. But different genres of e-history get seen in different ways, namely: (1) by being crowd-sourced; (2) by exploiting digital nostalgia; (3) by going viral; (4) by being visually arresting; (5) by being newsworthy; (6) through storytelling; and (7) via AI. The development of these mechanisms forms a loose chronology with the rise in popularity of different platforms. In other words, as new platforms or trends emerged, generating online enthusiasm and funding, new forms of e-history emerged along with them that sought to leverage the new technologies in order to gain visibility and influence. Piece-by-piece we will assemble this e-history universe—from Wikipedia to social networks to artificial intelligence—charting how it grew and unpacking its ramifications. In the short span of 20 years, our collective understanding of the past has evolved from crowd-sourced Wikipedia entries to history content generated by machines. Two decades into the new century, we are saddled with a sprawling and chaotic e-history universe we were not intentional about creating. Such a universe cannot be unmade, its consequences destined to shape our relationship with history for decades to come.

Finally, we'll examine the consequences of e-history for our understanding of the past. In conversation-after-conversation with students, journalists, friends and relatives, increasingly people expect to encounter—and deem valuable—historical information that adheres to e-history's conventions, often without realizing it. e-history has re-wired our brains and reconfigured which histories we feel are worth our attention and which are not: a remedy for boredom, a shortcut to understanding, in service of a brand or agenda, formulaic, emotional, symbolic, user-centric, novel, surprising and a relief from the history classroom. Quality of evidence, strength of argument and soundness of interpretation matter less to e-history's visibility than its conformity to a set of conditions. With so much content to sift through, it becomes increasingly onerous for Web users to expend the effort to search beyond what is immediately accessible. Once e-history has captured our attention as a good-enough source of historical information, the effort to dig deeper becomes inhibiting. One tech analyst admitted that e-history can be a gateway to further exploration of a subject, but that exploration will always be online, not in a book.[21] A podcast producer told me that when something historical piques his interest, he will not search for a book but rather go to YouTube to find something "bite-sized" to learn more.[22] An entrepreneur noted that even when he does try to read a scholarly journal article, he loses interest after the first two pages.[23] One study found that people who watched a television show about history were not likely to further research the topic.[24] In their book *Going Viral*, Karine Nahon and Jeff Hemsley argue that in a world of information overload, people regularly engage in "satisficing" on the Web. When faced with time and attention constraints, people will not seek perfect solutions but rather solutions that are good enough.[25] e-history produces a "satisficing" effect on users, a feeling that the user has a good-enough grasp of history in order to participate in whatever debate may be happening at the moment—whether it be about Donald Trump, Brexit, Confederate monuments or Black Lives Matter. Amid terabytes of historical information, and in an era of constant demands on people's time and attention, e-history becomes a proxy for all history.

In the end, debates over e-history are, at their core, debates over values, applicable to history as they are to journalism, science and other ways of knowing things about the world. If professional history continues to be disrupted by e-history, does that mean we will lose any grip on the past we may once have had? Do disciplines such as professional history have an intrinsic value to society, or does their value depend on extrinsic factors such as views, clicks and shares? Who should be entrusted to speak about certain topics, and what role do the platforms play in determining which voices get heard? These are arguments about power as much as they are about content: the power to set agendas, the power to shape society in one's image, the power to determine what we know and what we do not, and the power to profit from the massive expansion of the Web into every aspect of our lives. History on the social Web is linked to these complex power struggles, which emerge and re-emerge in different contexts. That tangled complexity informs the history we see on our phones, computers and tablets each day, even if we do not realize it.

Prior to the social Web, history (for some) may have been a retreat from the outside world, a quiet escape into a book, museum or classroom where knowledge was curated in an orderly and chronological fashion. That, in itself, is a form of nostalgia; history has long been sharply political and fiercely contested, any tidiness a product of linear gate-keeping forms of media such as books, newspapers and documentary films. Today, we are constantly surrounded by competing pasts clamoring for our attention, a scattered and messy array of stars and planets, each of varying sizes and brightness, the sheer multitude making it harder, not easier, to know which are the most significant and what the contours are of the broader universe may be. Chronology becomes nearly impossible as information gets flattened and communicated on the Web all-at-once. We catch tidbits of historical information as they fly by, clutching onto familiar patterns and premises that deliver a satisfying jolt of emotion or self-affirmation, that offer a "good enough" understanding in order to make a comment about a trending topic. As is clear from the PragerU video, e-history that adheres to, and aligns with, the values of the social Web stand a greater chance at visibility than the e-history that do not. To know why, we must better articulate what e-history is and where it came from.

e-History: Not Quite History and Not Quite the Past

e-history solves a problem, namely, how do you transpose the study of history into the Web and social media? The problem exists because, at heart, the values that underpin the professional discipline of history are at odds with the values that underpin the social Web. Professional history is an expert-centric, always-evolving intellectual pursuit that is time-consuming and rests on its intrinsic value. The social Web is a user-centric, data-driven commercial enterprise that is instantly gratifying and privileges extrinsic value. That clash creates the conditions for *e*-history to emerge.

The discipline of history is, at its core, **expert-centric**. This applies in the Ivory Tower, museums, national parks, government or think tanks. Professional history places the expert at the center of communicative power: professors teach and students learn. Curators make museum exhibits and museum-goers visit them. Park rangers give tours and visitors ask questions. Scholars determine the merits of what other scholars write, and young scholars must read a selection of senior scholars in order to participate in scholarly debates.[1] While all these exchanges are fluid and dialectical, a certain hierarchy ensures that professional methods, principles and standards of interpreting the past are met and maintained. Professional history must uphold expectations of accuracy, seriousness, rigor and sophistication, and gate-keeping ensures that only those with the proper qualifications and deference to prior scholarship assume central positions of power. "It's important that we talk about the war actually knowing something about it," to quote one Civil War historian. "Scholars and

© The Author(s), under exclusive license to Springer Nature
Switzerland AG 2022
J. Steinhauer, *History, Disrupted*,
https://doi.org/10.1007/978-3-030-85117-0_2

smart people should be out in front."[2] Not all arguments are valid, and not all opinions are equal[3]; "scholars and smart people" determine which is which.

Scholars and smart people are necessary because professional historians see history as an **always-evolving intellectual pursuit**. Historical arguments are continually re-assessed as new evidence emerges and new information comes to light. The past is a messy and complex place, the examination of which provides no clear answers, no easy solutions, no obvious lessons, no repeating laws and no simple morals. This is particularly relevant to tidy myths created by nation-states. Historians are wary of state-sponsored narratives and take pride in debunking state-sanctioned myths (though historians have myths they tell themselves). To the professional historian, history is a dangerous minefield that requires sophisticated critical thinking to navigate. Conclusions must be couched in careful, qualifying, sometimes abstruse, language.

For these reasons, professional history is **time-consuming**. Writing a book or creating a museum exhibit can take several years. The gathering, processing and synthesizing of historical evidence is slow and laborious and the pay-offs are never immediate. A historian can travel long distances at great expense to view archival materials, only for those materials to not make it into the final analysis. Travel costs, work hours, research time, writing time, editing time, review time and publication time all factor into producing a book, article or exhibit that may or may not ever be seen by many people. History education is also time-consuming: to earn a history PhD can require 24 years of schooling.[4] Students must "learn the particular and distinctive ways historians think ... and their special method for working with such information," to quote one historian.[5] As such, professional history is inefficient and difficult to scale; it scales when historians are compelled to become more prolific by their peers or when funding allows for the minting of new historians.

For all these reasons, historians consider history to be **intrinsically valuable**. History derives its importance from the fact that it exists, an inherently valuable process that produces inherently valuable outcomes. Professional history offers understanding, moral clarity and a foundation for citizenship. "The study of history justifies itself in so far as it assists reason to work and improve itself," to quote one historian.[6] History can be done in service to larger causes, be it education, democracy, human rights or social justice, but its core contribution is understanding as accurately as possible what occurred in the past. History is considered to be something that few of us know well, and whose value must be re-stated year after year. As such, history advocacy comprises a huge amount of history communication, the premise being that knowing a lot of history confers a certain wisdom. We ignore history at our peril, even if we cannot always articulate what that peril may be.

The social Web, on the other hand, has a very different set of foundational values. The social Web, at its core, is **user-centric** as opposed to expert-centric. One does not have to be an expert or a recognized authority to publish on the social Web. Everyone is encouraged to speak, contribute, comment and form their own opinion regardless of their credentials or expertise. On TikTok, Twitter, Facebook, Reddit, YouTube or Wikipedia, the permission of a supervisor or subject-matter expert is not required to upload and press "submit." In fact, the opposite is often foundational to the platforms' existences. Wikipedia co-founder Jimmy Wales once reportedly said that "people who expect deference because they have a PhD and don't want to deal with ordinary people tend to be annoying."[7] Clubhouse co-founder Paul Davison stated that on his platform, "Everyone is an equal, regardless of expertise."[8] One tech entrepreneur stated in a Clubhouse chat that she does not agree with "judging people on their merits to discuss something based on how well-read they are in a certain subject area."[9] User-generated content is essential to the social Web's philosophies and business models, and the platforms are continually adjusting to facilitate greater participation. As one Silicon Valley insider told me, "It's a buffet, not a French restaurant."[10]

Users are essential because nearly all the major Web 2.0 platforms are, at heart, **data-driven commercial enterprises**. Platforms such as Google, Facebook, Twitter and Instagram are, for all intents and purposes, advertising businesses. Advertising accounts for 87 percent of Google's revenue and 98 percent of Facebook's.[11] Even Wikipedia had aspirations to sell ads at the outset.[12] The platforms harvest enormous amounts of data from users and, leveraging algorithms, learn over time what features, products, people and content resonate with them. The algorithms deliver the optimized results as efficiently as possible. As it is operationally inefficient to have humans review each piece of content, elements of moderation are sacrificed in order to make the machinery work. The goal is to find the shortest distance between two (or more) points. Data and math, coupled with engineers and machines, can make huge breakthroughs, solve global problems, reduce costs, lower obstacles, find answers, push boundaries, achieve audacious goals and disrupt the status quo. (Data can also create new problems or worsen existing ones.)

At the operational and content levels, then, the social Web is **instantly gratifying**, as opposed to the professional practice of history, which is laboriously time-consuming. Search results appear immediately. The most relevant pages are meant to be the first that you see. Publishing can be done with a simple click. The goal of the platforms is to reduce the friction to create, consume and interact, and deliver gratification and pay-off each time. Because that's how the social Web has been designed, the most effective content on the Web adheres to this logic: delivering what we want quickly in ways that will keep us engaged. Tactics to create such content include using elements of surprise, effective storytelling, being aspirational or inspirational, stimulating our emotions, being provocative, personal, accessible, casual, unique, outlandish, beautiful, straight-to-the-point, delivering clear and easy answers or being relatable to the current news cycle. Accuracy or the agreement of experts is not a necessity. Social media platforms and Web searches, then, are a dialectical creation between the user and the machine: we give the algorithm information as to what content might cause us to spend more time on the platform, and, in turn, the algorithm attempts to maximize our time on the platform by leveraging our data to deliver content we'll engage with. We influence the algorithm and the algorithm influences us. The platforms and users are in an iterative process to become more efficient.

For all these reasons, content on the Web is **extrinsically valuable** as opposed to intrinsically valuable. A certain "market logic" underpins all Web 2.0 platforms, the belief that the number of consumers using a product ultimately determines its value.[13] Social media companies argue they are neutral distributors of user-generated content that do not endorse particular types of content over others.[14] Content on the Web gets elevated in our feeds based on its virality and popularity, not through quality judgments by select individuals (though there are exceptions). Users upvote or downvote content on Reddit; like, love or share on Facebook; retweet or comment on Twitter; view, favorite or skip on YouTube; or manipulate page-rankings on Google. These signals are measured by the algorithms to determine what we see next. What is determined to be the most optimal result by the algorithm is based on what is measurable, and is computed based on how we engage with the platforms, the data collected about us and the networks we are in. No independent arbiter can evaluate each piece of content for its veracity, accuracy or integrity. When millions of people collectively engage with content, it becomes publicly valued information.

Infusing professional history into the social Web, then, entails transplanting an expert-centric, always-evolving intellectual pursuit that is time-consuming and perceived to be intrinsically valuable into a user-centric, data-driven commercial enterprise that has been purposefully designed to be instantly gratifying and extrinsically valuable. It's a bit like placing a square peg into a round hole; the values and incentives are totally misaligned. To communicate history successfully online, then, means adapting to conventions and formulas that are best-suited for the social Web and how users have been conditioned to receive and respond to information.

Enter, *e*-history. *e*-history leverages the social Web to deliver information about the past in a manner that is purposefully designed to reach our eyes. It harnesses the mechanics of the social Web to become visible while using particular tactics to keep us engaged. For example, the tactic of surprise works well to attract user attention and keep readers reading. Scores of *e*-history content, then, rely on the conceit of surprise to gain visibility within our feeds: "10 Surprising Civil War Facts" from the HISTORY Channel website; "7 Truly Odd Historical Facts That I Had A Hard Time Believing Were Real" from Buzzfeed; and "125 Mind-Blowing Historic Facts & Trivia That Are Almost Too Weird to Be True" from Parade.com are three examples.[15] Sometimes the surprises are explicit; other times they are more subtle. It may be surprising, for example, to see a soldier in full dress uniform deliver a lecture about the Civil War. As creators of *e*-history—be they professional historians, history enthusiasts, news corporations or disinformation agents—learn what we respond to and what the platforms incentivize, the more those types of *e*-history get made in hopes that they will generate views, likes, clicks and shares. The critic Lewis Mumford wrote that the technologies of the twentieth century had "come to control the options available to us, making us more and more like cogs that allow our machinery to operate as it has been designed to operate."[16] Similarly, the social Web forces us to create content that is best optimized for its designs, including *e*-history.

e-history exists along a spectrum between "the past" and "history." Though these terms are often used interchangeably, there is a distinction. As you read this sentence, you are in the present. Now? The reading of that previous sentence is in the past. When you bought this book? Also, the past. "The past" comprises the infinite number of events that have occurred right before this very moment. "History," on the other hand, deals with *interpretations* of the past. Professional historians interpret the past based on the evidence they collect through research and present those interpretations to each other and the public in the form of scholarly arguments.[17] As John H. Arnold writes in his book, *History: A Very Short Introduction*: "History is above all else an *argument*. It is an argument between different historians; and, perhaps, an argument between the past and the present, an argument between what actually happened, and what is going to happen next. Arguments are important; they create the possibility of changing things."[18]

At one extreme, then, *e*-history resurfaces one of the infinite number of events that have occurred in "the past." This re-packaging of past events for consumption on the Web is done by historians, journalists, activists, hobbyists, teachers, high school students, Russian disinformation agents and artificial intelligence. Sometimes it is extremely difficult to determine who did it, raising numerous ethical and practical questions. What happens if a piece of *e*-history content about the past that is factually accurate turns out to be created by a Russian disinformation agent? What happens when an algorithm recommends *e*-history content by a professional historian, but subsequently recommends content created by a malicious actor? Should *e*-history from a PragerU video be removed from the Web if professional historians object to it—even if such content features another professional historian? Who should determine who has the authority to speak on certain subjects? *e*-history connects to broader debates around expertise, authority, content moderation and how to make sense of what we see on the Web each day.

At the other extreme, *e*-history can communicate professional "history," a.k.a. a scholarly argument based on evidence and rooted in historiography. Indeed, a portion of the *e*-history universe comprises such content created by professional historians. During the past 25 years, an entire subfield of digital history emerged that used digital tools to make scholarly arguments and answer historiographical questions.[19] While some *e*-history directly cites professional scholarship, other *e*-history purposefully distances itself from it—even positioning itself as an antidote to it. The "Crash Course" video series created by John and Hank Green was purposefully created to disrupt the traditional history lecture, which was perceived to be boring and lacking creativity, and to make free education online a legitimate and authoritative source.[20] Similarly, Khan Academy, created by financial analyst Sal Khan, sought to disrupt history education with online courses in American history, world history and art history. Both series became Web sensations; a friend of mine confessed in 2016 that she had "loved John Green's Crash Course world history videos"[21] and a Progressive activist exclaimed on Twitter in 2020, "I love Crash Course!" because the videos helped her pass an exam.[22] Such user enthusiasm generated hundreds of millions of views and funding for both projects.[23] In the case of Khan Academy, there were challenges to the accuracy of his videos, particularly in the sciences, where at least two of the videos got their physics wrong.[24] Yet, despite objections from some academics, these e-history videos succeeded in capturing people's attention during a period when professional history experienced vast declines in student enrollments.[25] Within the academy, hierarchy and peer-review would have adjudicated whether a novelist (Green) or a financial analyst (Khan) could speak with authority on certain historical subjects. Such a logic prevents material that is not sufficiently vetted from being published and distributed widely. But the social Web operates under a different logic. If millions of users enjoy a particular piece of e-history, it has the capacity to become an authoritative and publicly valued source of education, even if scholars deem it inaccurate or oversimplified.

As we'll see throughout this book, the trope that e-history is a reprieve from professional history re-appears across the social Web. This evinces an important aspect to e-history's success, namely, the stereotypes and perceptions of history by the public at-large. The Frameworks Institute found great antipathy toward history classes,[26] and in my own interviews people described professional history as "stodgy," "stuffy," "boring," "not relevant" and "joyless."[27] In a very Silicon Valley fashion, then, e-history purports to solve the problem of bland history lessons by removing them from the clutches of experts, dusty books, inaccessible archives and stale classrooms. If offline history is stodgy, e-history is stimulating. If offline history is didactic, e-history is tinged with emotion and human interest. If offline history takes effort to penetrate, e-history is effortless to retrieve. If history content is lengthy and nuanced, e-history delivers quick and satisfying answers. Like so much of the social Web, e-history promises a good-enough level of understanding as efficiently as possible.

As all media incur costs to make (money, time, effort), so much of e-history is also commercially motivated. e-history is often less concerned with the creation of new knowledge than it is in re-packaging existing knowledge into an efficient social product in order to advance a personal, political, ideological or commercial agenda. It leverages the past to sell something: a book, a product, a person, a brand, an institution or a discipline. To do so, *e*-history must attain visibility, which requires a sustainable business model that generates fresh content, repeated user interactions and can compete with the deluge of other online material on our screens each day. Web users are ultimately consumers on social platforms; history is another product they either choose to consume or ignore. Because the social Web is, at heart, a commercial enterprise that has evolved to privilege the symbolic value of products, the most visible *e*-history is produced as a sign and is meant to be in conversation with other signs. It is from its symbolism that it derives its value. The *e*-history that is best-suited to a particular platform—is best in conversation with other signs within the same online environment—will become the most visible in the feed, what venture capitalists and entrepreneurs describe as a product-market fit.[28] The most engaging *e*-history must always be, at heart, a *transaction*, precisely because the Web has been designed to always be taking us somewhere else. As we'll see, celebrated *e*-history creators are glorified by the press akin to entrepreneurs and celebrities: devising (or stumbling upon) a formula to grab users' attention, generate more transactions and induce the click.

Finally, the most visible *e*-history is user-centric. Like the Web itself, *e*-history content is predicated on giving the user control in how she navigates the past, offering the user ability to hop from place-to-place or from hyperlink-to-hyperlink as she chooses. *e*-history is fragmentary, not confined to the linear chronology or epistemic authority of a textbook, lecture, syllabus or museum exhibit. Scattered pieces of information from the past are used to construct digestible social products. *e*-history scours the record of the retrievable past to find the remarkable, surprising, unexpected, extraordinary, controversial and confrontational in order to create the most compelling Web content.

Across multiple years and platforms, the *e*-history that has reached our eyes and shaped our understanding of the past has been user-centric, commercially motivated, instantly gratifying and extrinsically valuable—because that content aligns best with the underlying values of the social Web. Content that was expert-centric, not commercially viable, time-consuming and relied on its intrinsic value struggled to achieve visibility. Yet, different types of *e*-history become visible in different ways. *e*-history can reach our eyes by:

(1) being crowd-sourced, what I will call the **crowd-sourced past**;
(2) delivering technologically induced nostalgia, what I will call **on-demand nostalgia**;
(3) going viral, what I will call the **viral past**;
(4) being visually arresting, what I will call the **visual past**;
(5) being newsworthy, what I call the **newsworthy past**;
(6) being a good story, what I will call the **storytelling past** and
(7) being generated by machines, what I will call **History.AI**.

These different mechanisms for achieving visibility and influence have emerged in a loose chronological order with the evolution of the social Web. In retracing that trajectory, we can begin to see how the *e*-history universe came to be, what values and assumptions underpinned it, how certain types of *e*-history were made, by whom, and why they appeared in our feeds. We can also begin to see why the abundance of *e*-history had little to do with advancing a better understanding of the past, and more to do with advancing particular agendas at particular moments in time. Those competing agendas, inundating the screens of hundreds of millions of Web users, have created a state of overwhelmingness and confusion as it relates to the past. It has also contributed to the subsuming of the values of professional history in favor of those of *e*-history.

The rise of Wikipedia in the early 2000s offers a useful starting point in this journey, as Wikipedia, in many ways, laid the foundation for the *e*-history that would come after it. The most significant contribution of Wikipedia was not a greater understanding of history. Rather, it introduced an important mechanism for *e*-history to become highly visible on the social Web: crowd-sourcing. That very concept placed the clash of values between professional history and the social Web right at its heart.

CHAPTER 3

The Crowd-Sourced Past

The crowd-sourced past is one mechanism that enables *e*-history to become visible on our screens. If enough Web users contribute to, or interact with, *e*-history, that can raise it to collective attention and grant it legitimacy and authority on the social Web. This follows one of the foundational logics of the Web, namely, that high volumes of transactions and interactions help to determine value. According to Web 2.0 logic, no content gets elevated solely for its intrinsic value. The number of consumers interacting or upvoting a piece of content ultimately determines its worth, regardless of its accuracy or veracity. When millions of people collectively participate in the elevation of *e*-history content, it becomes highly visible online and deemed publicly valued information.

The emergence of Wikipedia in the early 2000s laid the groundwork for the crowd-sourced past in many ways, as well as other characteristics of *e*-history that would emerge on subsequent platforms: user-centric, commercially viable, instantly gratifying and extrinsically valuable. Yet, before delving into Wikipedia and its consequences for *e*-history, it's important to differentiate between the "World Wide Web" and the "Internet," as well as clarify the "social Web" and "Web 2.0." Just as "the past" and "history" are used interchangeably yet have different meanings, so, too, do the "Web" and the "Net" have distinctions even when used as synonyms. To paraphrase Tim Berners-Lee, who is often credited with formulating the concept of a World Wide Web while at CERN in the late 1980s, on the Internet you find computers; on the Web, you find information. The Web

J. Steinhauer, *History, Disrupted*,
https://doi.org/10.1007/978-3-030-85117-0_3

could not exist without the Internet, but it is much more than computers sending instructions to each other. The Web comprises an abstract, imaginary space wherein all online documents, sounds, videos and information reside.[1] The Internet connects devices; the Web connects information via hyperlinks. Hyperlinks are formative because they allow information to be presented in a manner that leads to other information, inducing "the click" as it were. Inherent in the purpose of communication on the Web is not to present a single piece of content but to use a piece of content as a pathway to another piece of content. In this regard, the Web allows the user to be proactive in shaping her own experience. The Web empowers the user not to have to read the entire article or watch the entire video if it does not hold her attention; the very structure of the Web encourages her to look elsewhere. The Web wants her to continue hopping from hypertext to hypertext. That is its promise of empowerment and also how it has been addictively designed.

The creation of the Internet and the Web have been well-documented in many books and articles. For the purposes of understanding e-history, recall the problem from the previous chapter that e-history aims to solve: the transposition of historical content onto the social Web. The early iteration of the World Wide Web—Web 1.0—was primarily read-only and non-interactive. It functioned more akin to books, articles, newspapers and magazines. Walter Isaacson, who was the head of new media for TIME, Inc. in the mid-1990s, recalled that when TIME.com launched on Web 1.0, "we and other media companies repurposed our print publications into Web pages to be passively consumed by our readers … the focus was not on discussions and communities and content created by users. Instead, the Web became a publishing platform featuring old wine—the type of content you could find in print publications—being poured into new bottles."[2]

History content operated similarly on Web 1.0. Early projects such as "American Memory" from the Library of Congress, launched in 1994, took physical materials and placed them onto the Web accompanied by text from scholarly experts such as would appear in books or card catalogs.[3] Visitors to the American Memory website had to submit a form in order to report an error or add a comment. History on the Web in the 1990s, then, retained the characteristics of history off the Web: an expert-centric, intellectual pursuit with a modicum of gate-keeping to ensure standards and accuracy, time-consuming to create and justified by its intrinsic value to society. Most of it was deliberately not crowd-sourced.

As blogs, wikis and social networking in the 1990s and early 2000s ushered in Web 2.0 and the social Web, it disrupted—and eventually replaced—those values with a new set. Wikipedia had this collision right at its core.

Wikipedia was preceded by Nupedia, a free online encyclopedia launched in 2000 by Jimmy Wales and Larry Sanger. Conceived as a potential rival to the Encyclopedia Britannica, Nupedia relied on the premise that any credible encyclopedia had to be overseen by experts.[4] Led by Sanger, a PhD in Philosophy, Nupedia had an advisory board of scholars who served as editors and a seven-step review process that vetted each article before it could be posted.[5] It proved remarkably inefficient. After 18 months the site had only two dozen entries.[6] Though Sanger and Wales wanted members of the broader public to contribute, that happened in very few instances. Experts held the communicative power; non-experts could only contribute at certain points. Most importantly for Wales, the project wasn't fun or exciting. Wales described contributing to Nupedia as "intimidating," "stressful" and like being "back in grad school."[7]

Meanwhile, a spin-off project called Wikipedia showed more promise. Launched in 2001 by Wales and Sanger, anyone could write, edit or contribute. Expertise was not required. Borrowing from the concept of the WikiWikiWeb, which had emerged a few years earlier, a wiki enabled people to create and edit in real time directly in a browser. Any user could change a published text, correct errors or expound on an idea. No single authority dictated what could or could not be said, and all changes were publicly viewable. Equally important, it was fun. "People would write something and come back later and find that their words had improved," recalled the designer of the wiki concept, Ward Cunningham. "That's pretty exciting."[8] Wales and Sanger applied that open and decentralized mindset to their encyclopedia project. Those without credentials would contribute as equally as those with credentials; very few, if any, contributors would be barred from writing, editing or commenting. Wikipedia would not be a site for scholars to publish original research or professional opinions, and would "feature very little attempt to exercise authority," to quote Sanger.[9] Launched in January 2001, Wikipedia had 600 articles by the end of the month, 1300 in March, 2300 in April and 3900 in May.[10] By summer 2001, the Wikipedia homepage was explicit in its ethos: a "collaborative project to produce a complete encyclopedia from scratch" in which "*anyone* can edit any page" (emphasis in original).[11] Within a year, 18,000 articles had been published.[12]

Wikipedia would eventually become the fifth most viewed website on the planet, while Nupedia would shut down in 2002.[13] From this outcome, the norms and values for future *e*-history would be forged: user-centric as opposed to expert-centric; viable as a business model; instantly gratifying; and the value of the project derived from extrinsic measurements as opposed to intrinsic factors. The clash of values between Wales and Sanger had a clear winner on the social Web: for a crowd-sourced encyclopedia to work, it had to facilitate as wide a participation as possible and be enjoyable for the participants. Submissions had to be instantaneous as opposed to time-consuming. It could not be gate-kept by experts. And it required a large volume of transactions in order to attract public and media attention, as well as advertising revenue and corporate funding.

The number of contributors mattered because Wikipedia and Nupedia needed business models to survive. Wikipedia originally launched as Wikipedia.com; the intention was to sell advertising. Ad revenue was essential because programmers and staff needed money to keep Wikipedia running, not to mention purchase server space. A lack of revenue was part of the reason why Sanger was let go from the project; the company could not afford to pay him.[14] As Wikipedia grew, Wales switched to a donation model and migrated the site to Wikipedia.org. The encyclopedia could be crowd-sourced and crowd-funded because so many people were involved. Nupedia, on the other hand, had no viable business model. It took too long to finish articles, the review process was clunky and inefficient, and there were insufficient funds to pay organizers. Nupedia spent $250,000 to generate a double-digit number of entries.[15] Recall, too, that for John Arnold, a central characteristic of professional history was argument. Nupedia's lengthy review process got bogged down by scholarly arguments. One Nupedia contributor's frustrations included how scholarly reviewers "wanted to argue forever about things."[16] The arguments that make historical scholarship an always-evolving intellectual pursuit led to Nupedia's demise as a product of the social Web. That process may have led to more rigorously researched end-products, but it meant fewer end-products.

Speed was part of Wikipedia's founding ethos; wiki comes from a Hawaiian word for "quick."[17] Each entry would not be a precise history vetted by experts before publication, but rather a good-enough entry published as quickly as possible that could subsequently be revised and improved. That allowed it to scale, and scaling was how the project became valuable. Web users, media outlets and funders flocked to Wikipedia because it was quickly scaling something that was novel and that people enjoyed. They ignored Nupedia as it maintained its faith in the intrinsic value of a time-consuming process that experts felt was necessary to attain the truest results. Wikipedia packaged elements of the past into digestible social products crowd-sourced by users that approximated—and in many cases drew upon—the scholarship of professional historians. It became the first platform on the social Web to feature vast amounts of user-generated historical content. Its value stemmed from large numbers of people engaging with it, not its accuracy or veracity.

Almost immediately, scholars and journalists debated whether Wikipedia entries were reliable and accurate enough, warning they could never replicate books or libraries. Historian Roy Rosenzweig wrote an article in 2006 titled "Can History Be Open Source?" wherein he encouraged professional historians to learn from Wikipedia's successes while at the same time described the site as "problematic," expressed concerns over misinformation in its entries and lamented how it more often than not reflected "popular, rather than academic, interests in history"[18] (i.e., not expert-centric). But Wikipedia proved a "good-enough" source of historical information to serve its users' purposes. One student studying for a history test using Britannica and Wikipedia found Wikipedia easier to use and sufficiently accurate.[19] Another user stated that he/she could do the equivalent of a year of study on World War II in about a week.[20] Users were "satisficing," to use Nahon and Hemsley's terminology, willing to trade rigor and thoroughness for speed and convenience. Wikipedia had rescued historical knowledge from the clutches of experts, deliberately eschewing the conventions of scholarly history in favor of establishing authority in a manner better-suited to what the World Wide Web was becoming. Wikipedia offered a user-centric, commercially viable, instantly gratifying and extrinsically valuable approach to writing and learning about the past based on a powerful idea: anyone could do it.

Studying and writing history has long been a hobby as well as a profession. To quote one historian, "If history was thought of as an activity rather than a profession, then the number of practitioners would be legion."[21] Yet, whereas prior to the social Web an amateur historian had limited ability to publish instantaneously and reach a wide audience, a platform such as Wikipedia allowed amateurs the ability to publish instantly and achieve as much, or more, visibility than the professionals. Responses from professional historians toggled back and forth between recognizing that such engagement could kindle more interest in history, to concerns that these emerging forms of history communication failed to address the harder and more critical questions that rigorous scholarship tackled. In 2008, an entire academic journal issue was devoted to historians debating the ethics of "Practicing History Without a License."[22] As we'll see throughout this book, the notion that history is something anyone can do is common to *e*-history—one reason why it poses such an existential threat to the history profession.

For all its hype and buzz, new contributions to Wikipedia actually peaked in 2006 and declined thereafter, its active contributors falling to less than a quarter of what they once were.[23] For the past decade and a half, the majority of Wikipedia contributions have been additions to existing articles.[24] Still, more than 6.2 million entries exist in the English-language Wikipedia, 10 percent categorized as history with tens of thousands more classified as biography.[25] And the influence of Wikipedia goes far beyond the number of entries. Today, crowd-sourced *e*-history from Wikipedia informs search engine results, maps, mobile apps, digital voice assistants, news stories, research projects, knowledge graphs, YouTube videos and a myriad of Web tools.[26] Flush with a $100 million endowment, the Wikimedia Foundation has launched a for-profit company that is selling developer tools to big technology companies such as Apple and Amazon, using Wikipedia to inform voice assistants and smart devices.[27] The *e*-history on Wikipedia is not solely visible on one of the world's most viewed websites; it informs the historical understanding of billions of people around the world by virtue of its diffusion across the Web. Wikipedia has also ushered in new notions of authoritativeness for a generation raised on the Web, its ethos and conventions established more than two decades ago shaping what information about the past we see and what we do not.

To better explain this, consider as a first example the case of historian Timothy Messer-Kruse. In 2012, Messer-Kruse attempted to update the Wikipedia page for the 1886 Haymarket riot, bombing and trial.[28] Messer-Kruse was an expert on American labor history and the Haymarket incident. Specifically, he wanted to correct a claim that prosecutors in the Haymarket case did not provide evidence that connected the defendants with the bombing. Messer-Kruse discovered this to not be wholly true; he cited testimony held by the Library of Congress, as well as his own peer-reviewed journal article, as evidence. His changes were rejected. He tried again and was rejected again. Two years later, after his book was published, he was rejected a third time. The wiki editors told Messer-Kruse that Wikipedia was not "truth." Rather, Wikipedia was "verifiability of reliable sources."[29] The purpose of a Wikipedia entry was not to arbitrate what was true but rather to document consensus about what could be verified. A Wikipedia entry reflected the accepted wisdom of the largest number of reliable sources. If, for example, a consensus among sources was that the sky was green in 1888, the Wikipedia article would state that the sky was green in 1888. If a single historian argued the sky was blue in 1888, that would not merit inclusion in the article, as it would not reflect a consensus of reputable sources.[30] In other words, crowd-sourced e-history *precluded* some knowledge about the past from entering the world's largest encyclopedia, even if it could be verified as accurate. Two modes of establishing authority were pitted against each other: a professional historian striving for the purest truth, believing that the expertise of a single person could supersede the accepted wisdom of dozens of non-experts, versus Wikipedians striving for an accurate reflection of current thinking, and who believed that knowledge about an incident could be too easily manipulated by a single viewpoint. In the case of Messer-Kruse, his discovery at the Library of Congress remained visible in his professional scholarship (likely read by few people) but obscured from the broader world.

As a second example, consider the case of Snowzilla. On January 22, 2016, at 12:49 p.m. author Andrew Lih tweeted that Wikipedians were actively covering an impending blizzard in the D.C. region nicknamed "Snowzilla."[31] Lih was actually late to the party; the initial entry for "Snowzilla" was created on January 20, 2016—two days *before* the storm. A Wikipedia administrator and weather enthusiast in California named Brenden (username "Cyclonebiskit") was already writing a history of the event before it occurred.[32] More than 15 Wikipedia contributors—including an aspiring meteorologist in Texas; a science aficionado in California; a self-described "I'm no expert editor" with an interest in anime; a political conservative with an interest in severe weather; a professional librarian; and a college student[33]—repeatedly updated the Snowzilla entry during the storm using reports by news outlets, government agencies and social media posts. This was, in effect, a new genre of historical writing: not quite journalism—which is sometimes dubbed the "first draft of history"—and not quite professional history, as John Arnold would define it. This was a hybrid of the two with an added element of being self-conscious during its creation that it would be viewed as a source of record moving forward.[34] These users collected information in real time and crowd-sourced a narrative about "the thing" before anyone had distance from "the thing" to assess its true impact. Its worthiness for being included in an encyclopedia derived from the fact that a sizable population of people who lived on the East Coast of the United States were talking about it.

Today, the "Snowzilla" entry, since renamed to "January 2016 United States blizzard," comprises more than 5300 words and 187 footnotes. More than 500 edits were made within the first month of the storm and nearly 1000 edits within the first year of the storm. Sixty-two edits were made in 2017; 22 edits were made in 2018; 9 edits were made in 2019; 23 edits were made in 2020; and 25 edits were made in 2021.[35] The further we get from Snowzilla, the less exceptional and noteworthy the storm seems. There have been hundreds of blizzards in the United States, and several have deposited more snow in the Northeast than this one. The Wikipedia entry for the blizzard of 1996, which dumped more snow on the East Coast (4 feet) than this storm 20 years later (3 feet), is far less extensive. But the 1996 storm occurred before the crowd-sourced past on the social Web. The Wikipedia page for the 2016 blizzard, for example, includes details such as the time of day that parking was suspended, the length of time that it took for snowplows to reach D.C.'s side streets, and the amount of time it took to clear the roads in Queens, New York. Minutiae such as this could be tracked down for the 1996 blizzard, but it would be done by traveling to local libraries or doing research in municipal archives. For blizzards of equal or greater severity further back in time, of which there are many, such information would require even deeper digging (pun intended). Being crowd-sourced before and during the event— the information gathered from what was immediately and readily available—resulted the appearance of the blizzard of 2016 being more significant than the blizzard of 1996. We see more about the 2016 blizzard than the 1996 blizzard simply because of where it happened, when it happened and how quickly and easily information about it could be found while it happened. Crowd-sourced *e*-history can produce a lot of *enthusiasm*, but not necessarily a lot of *significance*.

These two examples (among many) surface questions about how judgments are made about what to include or exclude in crowd-sourced *e*-histories. Just because there is more information about an event does not make that event more or less significant to the human experience. The 2016 blizzard and the decisions by mayors and governors seemed consequential at the time—especially to those directly affected by it, which happened to include the major media centers of New York and Washington, D.C. Years later they feel remarkably trivial. That this storm would have a 5500-word Wikipedia page with 187 footnotes seems almost laughable. More information does not mean better histories. There remains a *quali-tative* aspect to historical writing, a level of editorial discernment and judgment that helps determine which details are significant and which are not, which merit inclusion in the narrative and which are extraneous. In the case for the blizzard of 2016, there was a crowd-sourced frenzy to gather information that resulted in the *inclusion* of extraneous details. It reflects what Rosenzweig cautioned in 2006, namely, that when Wikipedia entries that are rushed into existence in response to whatever is igniting public controversy at that instant, they are more about staking a claim in the present than they are about understanding with fidelity and rigor what may have occurred in the past.[36] In the case of Messer-Kruse's edit, the crowd-sourced enthusiasm to hold firm to the ethos of the platform resulted in the *exclusion* of an important detail about the past. In both instances, the effects of crowd-sourced *e*-history are not a better under-standing of past events, but to deeper embed the values and mores of the social Web into our knowledge of history.

The cases of Haymarket and Snowzilla may seem innocuous. But what happens when crowd-sourced historical narratives have darker agendas? In Japan, online forums such as 2chan, which launched in 1999,[37] have become havens for right-wing and nationalist groups called the "Net Far Right," or the *netto uyoku*. Debates about Japanese history—Japanese empire, the Nanjing Massacre, World War II, the dropping of the Atomic bomb or Japanese colonialism—are a large part of *netto uyoku* conversa-tions, the group opposing histories that do not reinforce ideas of Japanese greatness.[38] The *netto uyoku* have effectively used the social Web to crowd-source their ideas about the Japanese past into the mainstream.

Japan's history has been fiercely contested since World War II. In the 1970s, conservative activists organized to require imperial-era names and dates in Japanese official documents, resulting in a new national law in 1979. The same activists helped revise Japan's constitution to remove a provision banning Japan from participating in wars. During the contested battle over "comfort women" that cast into the spotlight Japan's role in sex slavery in Korea, a Society of the History Textbook Reform emerged in the 1990s that advocated for the positive aspects of Japanese empire. This movement spawned organizations such as the Association of the Families of Victims Kidnapped by North Korea and the National

Association for the Japanese Kidnapped by North Korea.[39] Scholar Tomomi Yamaguchi writes that with the rise of the social Web, this activism shifted online. Web campaigns called for members to elevate nationalist or xenophobic *e*-history content on social networking sites. These campaigns have crowd-sourced their ideas into public consciousness, finding their way into books, comic books, mass media, street demonstrations and national politics. Like contributors to the Snowzilla article, the *netto uyoku* members are ordinary citizens: a high school graduate, a beauty parlor owner, a bank employee, a truck driver, a bar owner, an electrical technician, a hostess and a high school student.[40] Critic Ogiue Chiki says that for many of these Japanese Internet users, the decision to engage in these forums hinged on whether attacking other individuals, groups or countries was "fun."[41] This is a darker side of the "fun" that Jimmy Wales and Ward Cunningham sought to engineer through their crowd-sourced platform. By manipulating the crowd-sourced mechanics of the Web, ideas about the past can go from fun and fringe to sinister and mainstream.

On crowd-sourced platforms such as Wikipedia, Reddit, Quora, 2chan and 4chan, crowd-sourced *e*-history rises to the top of our feeds each day because the social Web privileges engagement, controversy and being noticed as opposed to being accurate. Perhaps these pieces of information come from a professional historian, a textbook, a journalist, an anecdote, a family member or a conspiracy theorist. There is a noble ethos to this model, a participatory and democratic form of creating the national narrative. It unwinds the tidier narratives of earlier eras crafted by a homogeneous set of writers. But it also permits ideas about the past that come from darker, more insidious corners of the Web to creep in; no rigorous peer-review process gate-keeps the publishing of material. In recent years, historians, archivists and librarians have worked to improve thousands of Wikipedia pages. Some institutions have instated Wikipedian-in-Residence programs and annual events support volunteers who add information about women and minorities that have been overlooked by Wikipedia contributors, as well as correcting biases and inaccuracies. Many Wikipedia entries now include a combination of academic and popular sources.

Yet, as a result of Wikipedia and similar sites, the crowd-sourced past has become an imprimatur of authority for a younger generation.[42] Evidence suggests that Generation Z views crowd-sourced forms of knowledge as more authoritative than the knowledge of a single expert. A 2018 article in *The Atlantic* reported on teens who used "flop" accounts on Instagram to discuss issues such as politics, social protest or breaking news. Teenagers found flop accounts to be "far more reliable because it could be crowdsourced and debated."[43] They did not trust information delivered by a single author; they assumed that any single author—a teacher, a professor or a journalist—had an agenda and was simply one person expressing an opinion. An interactive forum such as a "flop" account (where users posted memes with socially incorrect opinions and debated them in the comments) allowed for ideas and information to be exchanged, crowd-sourcing its way toward truth. One teenager said, "Flop accounts have a lot of people fact-checking each other instead of just depending on one source giving us information ... we all have to do research and it's a lot of people completing these things together, not just one person, which makes us trust it more."[44]

Within these flop accounts there were administrators—teenagers from anywhere in the world—who investigated claims that appeared to be false or that got flagged by another user. If claims could not be backed up, they could be taken down. This raises questions about how the administrators debunked claims, as well as what counted as an authoritative source if journalists and professors were not to be trusted. One might surmise that Wikipedia would be a trusted source, which would mean one crowd-sourced platform was fact-checking another. But the underlying ethos of where authority resides was consistent. Authority emerged from the crowd working through a series of facts and counter-facts together in real time to emerge with a consensus that could be considered authoritative. Single authors were simply another voice in the crowd, the deference to experts that Wikipedia founder Jimmy Wales abhorred now firmly entrenched within society.

I found this to be consistent with my own interactions with high school and college students. In summer 2019, I spoke to a group of interns at the Foreign Policy Research Institute. I asked the students how they came to decide what was authoritative. Without prior consultation, each student independently said consensus among dozens of sources was the standard they employed. No student suggested she would rely on a single scholar or sole subject matter expert, no matter how qualified. "If you're used to deferential treatment at your home institution, you'll be treated like every-body else in the Wide Open Internet," one commenter wrote in response to Messer-Kruse in 2012.[45] Credibility must be earned in the broader mar-ketplace of ideas alongside other users, some of whom may know far less about the subject. Ideas must be crowd-sourced to the top of the feed in order to be accepted. Experts must attract followers in order to claim authority. Having an advanced degree does not guarantee your ideas will merit special consideration. Being crowd-sourced on the social Web can lend the information *more* authority and visibility; whereas being a solitary expert can grant it *less.*

Not surprisingly, historians, academics and journalists—all of whom have sensed their single-author authority to be endangered by the social Web—have spoken out against this in recent years, citing the dangers of a "post-truth" and "post-expertise" world. Professor Tom Nichols's 2017 book and essay in *Foreign Affairs* on the "death of expertise" warned that being dismissive of subject matter experts could lead to the end of democracy itself.[46] These models of authority engendered by the social Web have made experts uneasy. To quote the Civil War historian from Chap. 1, "scholars and smart people" should be out in front—except on Wikipedia they are not, a purposeful choice dating back to its creation.

Crowd-sourced e-history on the social Web has made professional historians another source of subjective opinion, blurring the distinction between a professional historian and an amateur one. The former's opinion may be more informed than the latter, but both have to duke it out in the marketplace of ideas before a consensus-based truth emerges. Mathematician Andrew Odlyzko has suggested that scholars should embrace this new normal, not fight it. After all, as Max Planck opined, and Odlyzko reminds, "a new scientific truth does not triumph by convincing its opponents and making them see the light, but rather because its opponents eventually die, and a new generation grows up that is familiar with it."[47] Eventually, the historians and journalists defending previous models of authority will pass, and today's youth will become adults for whom consensus-forged truth will be the norm. That may already be the case.

Wikipedia entries, then, have been foundational to the formation of the broader e-history universe, an early barometer of debates around authority, judgment, expertise and accuracy that would continue to play out across the social Web over the ensuing two decades. Wikipedia established foundational aspects of e-history that would become hallmarks on future platforms: user-centric, an antidote to professional history, a relief from the tyranny of experts, requiring a sustainable business model and valuable for its attributes, not its accuracy. Crowd-sourced e-history in the early years of Web 2.0 played an enormous role in what has been learned about the past online in subsequent years. Still, as Wikipedia entries peaked in 2006 and began to decline in 2007, a new paradigm-changing website was already on the rise: Facebook, which had 12 million users in 2006 and 58 million users in 2007.[48] With Facebook came entire new forms of *e*-history that would achieve online visibility through customized mini-doses of nostalgia, packaged into appealing and digestible social products, ushering in a new form of *e*-history that would massively expand across the Web.

CHAPTER 4

Nostalgia on Demand

On-demand nostalgia packages moments from the past into micro-doses of sentiment in order to gain visibility in our feeds. Targeted toward individuals or groups, on the spectrum between "the past" and "history" along which *e*-history exists, on-demand nostalgia resides well in the camp of "the past." It has little, if anything, to do with professional history, and in many ways is antithetical to it. Yet, *e*-history promises to rescue the past from the clutches of experts, and like Wikipedia, micro-doses of nostalgia offer an instantly gratifying and satisfying jolt of emotion that provides a good-enough understanding of a past event or phenomenon. The rise of social networking in the early and mid-2000s, particularly on Facebook, made delivering these on-demand "historical emotions"[1] easier and easier. They became an effective, powerful and profitable mechanism to package the past for broad consumption on the social Web, nowhere more evident than the Facebook app, Timehop.

In the summer of 2010, Jonathan Wegener thought he had the next "killer product."[2] It was called Friendslist and it would be the Craigslist for private groups. If one friend needed a place to live, and another had a spare bedroom, a match could be made through a post on Friendslist. Wegener—a Web developer who majored in neuroscience, sociology and marketing at Columbia University—and his friend Benny Wong applied to the seed accelerator Tech Stars. They quit their jobs and for six months developed, built and tested their concept. Every iteration fell flat. Asking users to port over their contacts to a new platform proved too

J. Steinhauer, *History, Disrupted*,
https://doi.org/10.1007/978-3-030-85117-0_4

cumbersome. Plus, it didn't scale; with so many types of posts (some private, some public), it became too messy and cacophonous. Friendslist folded.

Along the way, however, Wegener and Wong came up with another idea. On the eve of a hackathon for the popular app Foursquare, they imagined an app that replayed a person's check-ins from prior year. Users could befriend their "ghosts" from check-ins past, then watch as their past selves checked into prior destinations on the day and time it happened. Occasionally, you and your ghost might be in the same place at the same time. Wegener recalls asking, "What's that saying 'Four score and something something ago?'" Wong allegedly replied, "Four Score and Seven Years Ago—it's from Abe Lincoln's Gettysburg address." They decided to call the app "Four SQUARE and Seven Years."[3]

4square&7yearsago started as an email service that sent people a list of places they'd visit one year earlier. The logo was an Abraham Lincoln mascot.[4] Users loved it; one graphic designer called it her "favorite hack!"[5] A TechCrunch writer called it a "delightful lesson in nostalgia."[6] Wegener told a reporter that users would wake up in the morning, read the email and have "nostalgic emotional experiences."[7] By the end of 2011, the app had thousands of users and had integrated with Facebook, Instagram and Twitter. They renamed it Timehop. In early 2012, they secured $1.1 million in funding.[8] They eventually raised $14 million and peaked at 6 million daily users.[9] In 2015, Facebook replicated the app and built its own digital nostalgia program, "On This Day." A year later, it had 155 million subscribers.[10] Today it lives on in the "Memories" tab.

Timehop was not interested in critical analysis of a user's past—or, for that matter, the creation of new knowledge that could be derived from examining a user's past. Like much successful *e*-history, Timehop was predicated on the re-packaging of existing information into an attractive digital product. To do so, Wegener and Wong devised a clever formula that leveraged the data supplied by the user. Yet, despite Timehop's distance from professional history—in its approach to the past and the credentials of its founders—Wegener and his team framed their product as a history app, employing the language of history and iconography of a famous U.S. president to bolster its cache. To be sure, there is a long tradition of using the gravitas of history to commercialize the past; as we'll see later in the book, many journalists describe themselves as historians in order to enhance their prestige and sell books. Wegener did similarly. As he and his team realized they'd stumbled onto a formula to engineer *e*-history success, he rebranded his product as a means of "recording, remembering and reconnecting around digital histories."[11] Wegener hoped the app would one day be the "ultimate way people experience their content history online."[12] Just as we had a "History" tab in our Web browser that automatically retraced a person's digital steps—so dubbed by computer scientists in the early days of the Web's development[13]—Timehop retraced a person's physical steps.

Timehop succeeded for several reasons. The product was user-centric, not expert-centric. Wegener and Wong did not envision a product that offered any substantive interpretation of a person's past by an expert. Rather, they used user data to resurface a series of past events tied to an anniversary. It was not a comprehensive set of past events, and no expert analyzed each Timehop post to assess what details it omitted or how it fit into a broader socio-political context. The app only pulled from the data that existed, meaning that numerous locations visited in a day that users did not check into were excluded. Like Facebook itself, Timehop was made possible by the data supplied by the individual user. As people communicated about themselves on social networks, Timehop leveraged that self-communication to create an on-demand *e*-history product about each person. It was, for all intents and purposes, a selfie—a representation of ourselves reflected back to us, a product well-suited for its time. During the period of Timehop's rising popularity, the word "selfie" was Oxford Dictionary's 2013 Word of the Year. Google reported in 2014 that people took approximately 93 million selfies per day just on Android phones.[14]

Communications scholars have argued that the selfie is, essentially, a form of on-demand nostalgia, a manner by which we sentimentalize a moment of our own past just after it happened.[15] It is also a hypertext, a form of communication that seeks to generate a click, mimicking the Web itself. It was the prototypical form of communication for the period when social media and Web 2.0 rapidly expanded into public consciousness: visual, highly personal, instantly shareable, meant to elicit a response, an act of exploiting and nostalgizing the past. Sociologist Manuel Castells termed this period the mass self-communication era, which encompassed the numerous ways that we communicated about ourselves, be it on Twitter, Facebook, YouTube and the rest. The mass self-communication era was, at its heart, about seeing ourselves reflected back to us.[16]

Timehop merged the on-demand desire to see ourselves reflected back to us with the changing incentives of the Facebook news feed. Starting in 2013, the Facebook feed became primarily focused on visual content. CEO Mark Zuckerberg reported at the time that almost 50 percent of content that users created was visual.[17] Photographs were the site's most popular content type, and users were moving toward, and responding positively to, bigger images, richer media and more immersive, vivid experiences—fueled by improvements to camera phones and faster mobile networks.[18] The response from Facebook was to increase the size and prominence of images on the platform. This satisfied advertisers, as it offered them new opportunities to insert vivid, attention-grabbing displays into our feeds and allowed Facebook to charge more for it. It also appealed to users; to quote the editor and founder of TechCrunch at the time, "Photos is quickly becoming my favorite place to go beyond the default feed … By showing you just images and no text or links, you don't have to consciously think as much. You just look at the pretty pictures."[19] Timehop had been sharing a URL with users that they would click on for their daily nostalgia dose. But as Facebook prioritized images, Timehop shifted to providing an image. That led to more likes, comments and engagement. The algorithm, in turn, delivered more Timehop content to more people.[20] Timehop hit its stride by leveraging these changes in Facebook's algorithm where users did not have to "consciously think as much." The Facebook algorithm aided significantly in Timehop's success.[21]

New social media technologies had created an "untapped opportunity in the past," and Wegener and Wong were not the only ones to recognize it.[22] A tech reporter noted that she saw a surge in products that leveraged the capabilities of user data, vivid imagery and desire to scroll through "pretty pictures" from the past.[23] That included services such as the photo-editing and archiving app Memento and the app Memolane, which promised users an "Internet Time Machine."[24] Using social media to resurface what occurred in the past on a given day soon emerged as an omnipresent e-history genre. The sub-Reddit /r/ThisDayInHistory was launched in May 2011—five months after 4square&7yearsago debuted—as a place to commemorate and discuss past events that took place on a particular day. Today it has more than 40,000 members.[25] A similar sub-Reddit, /r/OldSchoolCool, launched in 2012 and today has more than 14 million members. It featured nostalgic photographs of people's parents and grandparents, intermixed with nostalgic photos of celebrities. An explosion of "On This Day" (#OTD) or "This Day in History" (#TDiH) content emerged on Twitter, including by historians, museums, journalists and other history communicators. PBS tweeted, for example, #OTD content about Harvey Milk on the anniversary of his assassination, and interns running the Twitter account of the National Historic Landmark's Program used the hashtag #OTD to mark historic events for an entire summer.[26] Twitter accounts such as @URDailyHistory, run by a man named Joe,[27] amassed more than 65,000 Twitter followers by tweeting a factoid about an event that occurred on that same day in a prior year, accompanied by an image.[28] The account @todayinamericanhistory was launched on Instagram in 2014, and YouTube channels such as Historrically began creating "On This Day in History" videos.[29] The homepage of Wikipedia featured a section called "On this day," which pulled history-related content from its pages. Websites such as HISTORY.com, historynet.com, onthisday.com, thepeoplehistory.com and brittanica.com each produced "On-This-Day" e-history content. (HISTORY eventually created a "History This Week" podcast.) Even Journalist Carl M. Cannon, the Washington Bureau Chief of RealClearPolitics, wrote a book called *On This Date: From the Pilgrims to Today, Discovering America One Day at a Time.* "Everybody is starting to realize that there's value in the past," Wegner said.[30]

Facebook realized it as well. The company began to make the past a centerpiece of its digital economy, foundational to its very business model. Recognizing Timehop's success, Facebook developed its own app called "On This Day" to remind its users of what happened on a particular day and allow them to re-share it.[31] TechCrunch reported that re-sharing of "On This Day" posts drove engagement and lock-in with Facebook's News Feed, which was also where people saw ads.[32] Facebook became a scroll of the immediate past served up as customized and individualized media packets—what you did yesterday, who you saw on this date last year. By re-packaging memories as new Web content, it engineered nostalgia for the recent and created a profound commercial advantage for the company.[33] Packaging our individual pasts as e-history content personalized to each of us was a purposeful business strategy to commodify our memories and increase our engagement with the site in order to generate more ad revenue. Users responded positively. One of my Facebook friends wrote, "These throwbacks are the best part of Facebook."[34]

The scholar Svetlana Boym has written about nostalgia in such a milieu as a "historical emotion," and that was precisely what the platforms were selling. They stimulated a yearning for an earlier time, fostering an emotional reaction as opposed to one that relied on critical thinking.[35] "Technology and nostalgia have become co-dependent," Boym wrote. "New technology and advanced marketing stimulate *ersatz* nostalgia—for the things you never thought you had lost—and anticipatory nostalgia—for the present that flees with the speed of a click."[36] This commodification and memorialization of the everyday was "linked to a wider consumption economy," in the words of scholar Yasmin Ibrahim, a method by which we acquire social capital as we memorialize aspects of our own existence.[37] The desires for self-validation, endorsement and enshrinement have been stimulated by the very technologies themselves.

Interest in the past, thus, felt like it grew exponentially during the late 2000s and early 2010s. Our desire to connect emotionally with the recent, relatable past was expanding each day through growing amounts of e-history content in our news feeds. That this occurred during a period when history enrollments were dropping and history's relevance was questioned points to the opposing value structures at work: historical emotions for various pasts versus critical engagement with them; user-centric pasts versus expert-centric historical scholarship; instantly gratifying pieces of digital content versus the always-evolving, time-consuming intellectual arguments of professional scholarship.

Providing on-demand historical emotions via the social Web proved to be a powerful combination, not solely commercially but also politically. Micro-doses of visual nostalgia in the Facebook news feed precisely targeted to individuals turned out to have real-world political consequences. Columnists have chronicled how digital nostalgia was central to the politics of the 2010s, with figures such as Donald Trump in the United States, Vladimir Putin in Russia, Recep Tayyip Erdogan in Turkey, Xi Jinping in China, Narendra Modi in India and Viktor Orban in Hungary promising their supporters returns to more glorious pasts.[38] It's no surprise that these figures successfully utilized social media in their paths to power; social media was practically built to stimulate nostalgic emotions. Technologically induced nostalgia played a major role in the Presidential campaign of Donald Trump. The slogan "Make America Great Again" was a direct appeal to American popular nostalgia, in addition to being a dog-whistle to strands of racism and bigotry. The same logic that informed Timehop—gather data from willing users and use it to create customized and attractive digital news feed products—informed how Cambridge Analytica engineered highly individualized and targeted campaign materials for then-candidate Trump during the 2016 U.S. presidential election. Cambridge Analytica began with a quiz on Facebook that users engaged with because it was fun and showed an aspect of themselves back to them. That data was used to build micro-targeting tools for political ads.[39] The strategy delivered to Facebook users "nostalgic emotional experiences" about how to make America great again and return the United States to a more glorious white and Christian past.

But perhaps nowhere were these vivid, emotion-stoking, targeted uses of the Facebook news feed more effective than in the Philippines. Rodrigo Duterte and his supporters used the Facebook news feed in 2016 (with Facebook's active assistance), and the prioritization of bigger, richer and more vivid imagery, to build a shrewd political messaging operation. That operation, according to campaign documents, was purposefully centered upon stoking the emotions of Filipinos through social media memes on Facebook.[40] It proved remarkably effective, catapulting Duterte from a long-distance challenger to President-elect. It was particularly potent in a nation where 97 percent of Internet users had Facebook accounts and the social Web served as the principal method by which politically engaged Filipinos consumed information.[41] Much like Wegener said about Timehop, the Duterte campaign engineered its products to leverage the changes to the Facebook algorithm and to grab valuable and visible real estate in the news feed.[42] Photographs and memes foregrounded within the feed, used to stimulate historical emotions, proved to be an incredibly potent tool for gaining political power. The strategy evolved from the very same mechanisms and seemingly harmless data collection and image prioritizations only a few years earlier.

Using social media to stimulate historical emotions was not just limited to right-wing politicians. The digital nostalgia for nationalism on the Right was countered by digital nostalgia for activism on the Left—particularly the women's suffrage movement and the Civil Rights movement. The deployment on social media of historical imagery from these periods were equally engineered *e*-history products that represented a significant portion of the social media response to nationalist politicians, particularly President Trump. Images of Civil Rights activists and Olympians Tommie Smith and John Carlos, Martin Luther King, Jr., John Lewis and Harriet Tubman circulated widely online throughout the Trump Presidency. These *e*-history social media posts by academics, activists and Progressives were calculated productions of nostalgia, meant to signify a direct lineage between contemporary resistance and past activism, as well as stimulate historical emotions among like-minded voters in service of contemporary political aims. The deployment of these on-demand nostalgic images in moments of intense political debate, which will be further analyzed in our chapter on the visual past, were, in essence, selfies—forms of self-communication intended to stimulate a response, and to signify to others where one stood in the American culture wars. That they had symbolic power and were dramatically composed offered them visibility, regardless of how accurate or appropriate they may have been to the current situation. And much like Timehop could only pull from the material about your life that it had available, these digital *e*-history products drew upon the photographic archives that were most readily available to them. That privileged a particular body of images, particularly from the Civil Rights era, a heavily photographed movement, and whose archives were more easily retrievable on the Web. As photographic archives from the twentieth century are faster to find and repurpose, that imagery got deployed on a fast-moving social Web in whatever political or media debate was occurring.

Boym, writing presciently in 2007, stated that the twenty-first century would be characterized by "the proliferation of nostalgias that are often at odds with one another."[43] Through Facebook and other platforms, we demonstrate online which pasts we believe we've descended from, and which past historical actors reveal something about us. These forms of *e*-history are more about seeing ourselves reflected back to us than critical examinations of the past. Scholar Ernest Sternberg has described this as people "personifying their virtues."[44] *e*-history becomes more visible on the social Web when it personifies our virtues to others.

Today, Timehop's website claims the company "created the digital nostalgia category."[45] Whether Timehop created this category or not, the app was foundational to it, part of a broader zeitgeist wherein on-demand nostalgia became a prolific and powerful tool on the social Web. The genre has grown to become a sizable portion of the *e*-history universe, deployed by journalists, hobbyists, corporations, museums, national parks and political operatives to use the past to achieve visibility and influence. The category continues to proliferate; in 2021, the genealogy company MyHeritage introduced Deep Nostalgia, a service that used deep learning to simulate how deceased relatives in old photographs may have moved, smiled or gestured. Similar to Timehop, the app relied on photographs contributed by users to generate a bite-sized rush of technologically induced nostalgia.[46] The promotional video for the project featured a deep fake version of Abraham Lincoln reciting (you guessed it): "four score and seven years ago."[47]

The social Web purposefully reflects the past back to us in order to instantly and efficiently stimulate powerful emotions and advance a commercial or political agenda. The combined effect is not a richer or more nuanced understanding of history, but rather the diffusion of "on-this-day" content across the Web advancing a myriad of personal, political and commercial agendas, dispersed and atomized so as to defy cohesion. Once the genre had proven to be effective in attaining visibility on one platform, it migrated to others such as Reddit, Wikipedia, YouTube and Twitter. But Wegener and Wong were not the only duo to recognize that vivid imagery from the past could be exploited to achieve commercial success. If the nostalgic past could not solely be popular but also go viral, it could build tremendous influence, social capital and economic success. The rise of Twitter in the late 2000s and early 2010s, its market capitalization peaking in 2013,[48] made that business model possible and brought the conflicts around *e*-history more fully into public view.

CHAPTER 5

The Viral Past

In 2014, Xavier Di Petta was 17 years old and living in a small town north of Melbourne, Australia. His friend, Kyle Cameron, aged 19, was a student in Hawaii. They met via YouTube when they were 13 and 15, respectively, and began to create social media content together. They built YouTube accounts and earned money off the advertising. They created Facebook pages such as "Long romantic walks to the fridge," which garnered more than 10 million "Likes," and sold the pages for profits. Eventually, Di Petta started a company, Swift Fox Labs, and hired a dozen employees. At one point, Swift Fox earned A$50,000 per month.[1] In July 2013, the duo created the Twitter account @HistoryInPics. By 2014, when they were profiled in *The Atlantic*, the account, which tweeted old photographs with one-sentence descriptions, had more than 890,000 followers.[2] Today, it has nearly 4 million.[3] It is not uncommon for @HistoryInPics tweets to get retweeted thousands of times and receive tens of thousands of favorites, circulating pictures from the past around the globe.

@HistoryInPics epitomized the viral past, a form of *e*-history that sparks a social contagion through a network and a natural next evolution of the *e*-history universe. The viral past combined a quick dose of nostalgia with the emerging business model of virality to create a form of *e*-history that could achieve massive visibility and influence on the social Web. If Wikipedia placed the amateur on equal ground with the expert, and Timehop nostalgized the user-centric past in order to gain visibility in our

© The Author(s), under exclusive license to Springer Nature Switzerland AG 2022
J. Steinhauer, *History, Disrupted*,
https://doi.org/10.1007/978-3-030-85117-0_5

news feeds, @HistoryInPics went one step further, leveraging public displays of social capital (retweets, favorites and followers) to power a business model predicated on sending evocative imagery from the past across social media at rapid speeds. In so doing, the account would set the stage for Twitter to become a hotly contested battleground for who deserved to speak about the past, and foreshadow how e-history would be deployed in the fierce political fights that would dominate the social Web.

The viral past shares the characteristics of other successful e-history: user-centric, commercially motivated, instantly gratifying and extrinsically valuable. But it became a distinct genre unto-itself as virality became a means to accumulate social capital online. YouTube videos and Facebook campaigns were already receiving praise and attention for "going viral" by the mid-2000s. This led to a realization: Web content could not only go viral once it was created, it could be designed to intentionally go viral from its inception.[4] Public acclaim, media attention, commercial success and political power could be seized by creating content that was purposefully designed to provoke rapid user-sharing within a short period of time, a cost-efficient and highly effective mechanism for leveraging the social Web to gain visibility and influence. e-history was no exception.

@HistoryInPics was actually preceded in this logic by @Retronaut. @Retronaut appeared on Twitter in 2009 with the promise that it could make "the past go viral." The account took old photographs from books, newspapers and archives, enlarged them, added eye-pleasing fonts and circulated them on the Web. @HistoryInPics perfected what @Retronaut began, and imitation accounts soon followed: @historypix, @HistoricalPics4, @VeryOldPics and dozens more. The dominant e-history on Twitter of the mid-2010s was purposefully engineered to achieve social contagion. Analysis with rigor and sophistication was irrelevant.

This quadrant of the e-history universe formed concomitantly with Twitter's ascendance. Launched in 2006, Twitter gained momentum in Silicon Valley after the SxSW festival in 2007. In 2008, Barack Obama's electoral campaign demonstrated Twitter's potential to win political power. In 2009, CNN and Oprah Winfrey joined the platform. By 2010, the combined money and influence of Silicon Valley, Washington, D.C., and Madison Avenue had made Twitter the hot new social network, valued at more than $1 billion.[5] Crucially, Twitter was proving itself to be good for Wall Street, too, more effective than Facebook in driving consumer spending.[6] By the mid-2010s, Twitter was at the frontlines in the competitions for commercial, cultural and political power. Because Twitter was so influential by the time @HistoryInPics arrived, the account sparked an even fiercer backlash from professional historians than Wikipedia had a decade earlier. By the end of the 2010s, though, professional historians would embrace the viral past as vigorously as they had fought against it, as it became clear how effective it could be in resisting President Donald Trump and his brand of Conservative politics.

A precise definition of virality will be central to our argumentation moving forward. In their book *Going Viral*, Karine Nahon and Jeff Hemsley define virality as, "a social information flow process where many people simultaneously forward a specific information item, over a short period of time, within their social networks, and where the message spreads beyond their own [social] networks to different, often distant networks, resulting in a sharp acceleration in the number of people who are exposed to the message."[7] Virality is not synonymous with popularity; a Wikipedia page may be popular but is unlikely to go viral. Though Timehop was popular among Facebook users, its posts rarely went viral, if at all. Popularity entails wide acceptance among a majority of people; virality concerns rapid dissemination across a particular time and space. Virality follows a sigmoid curve: information spreads slowly at first, then speeds up, then plateaus and slows again.[8] One study looked at 106 million tweets and found that half of all retweets happened within the first hour and that 75 percent of retweets occurred within the first day.[9]

It is this rapid dissemination in a short amount of time that signals to the algorithm that users are responding to a piece of content. This, in turn, boosts the visibility of the content and pushes it across broader segments of users. Platforms such as Twitter tend to create like-minded clusters of like-minded people, the bonds among them forged by common interests. Virality spreads information from one cluster to another. Weak ties between clusters allow the information to spread.[10] Information moving rapidly from cluster to cluster via weak ties creates the effect of virality. An ability to manipulate information across clusters can, thus, grant you visibility and credibility as an effective communicator and authoritative source of information. Virality can lead to personal, commercial and political opportunities. Virality becomes a pathway to power.

For the viral past to succeed, then, it must create a distinct social media product that multiple users across clusters will simultaneously forward within and beyond their networks in a short period of time. The content, therefore, must be *user-centric*, that is, it must provoke the user to take an action or feel an emotion: wonder, amazement, fear, outrage and so on.

Such calculations were articulated by @HistoryInPics co-creator Xavier Di Petta in a TEDx talk he delivered in 2015. Di Petta developed a three-step formula to determine which pictures would be most likely to achieve virality: (1) Does this photo invoke any kind of emotion? (2) Would I make this photo my iPhone screensaver? (3) If the answers were no, it was not worth sharing.[11] @HistoryInPics intentionally selected images that would provoke the user into action. If the image could reveal something about the user—not about history—@HistoryInPics suspected it might go viral. On Twitter, any tweet can be easily retweeted. Yet, Twitter users are quite selective in who they retweet.[12] That's because retweeting, like the selfie, concerns self-presentation and how we want others to perceive us. The decision to retweet is, thus, based on *social* factors, not *technical* ones, that is, *what the information says about us.*

In the case of @HistoryInPics, the question was whether the image said something about *me*, the user? Did it say that I was cool, intriguing, artsy or that I had a particular attitude about something? Did it reveal something about my politics, my identity, my background or my heritage? Would I make this photograph my iPhone screensaver? The viral tweets from @HistoryInPics represented thousands of people within a short window of time determining that an image and its corresponding caption were cool enough, artistic enough, interesting enough or surprising enough that it would reflect well upon them—or represent something meaningful about them to retweet it. It was an act of self-communication.

Chris Wild devised a similar formula for @Retronaut. He recalled:

> With the help of my friends Amanda Uren and Simon Mallindine, I posted around 40,000 Retronautic photographs onto the site in "capsules"—small collections, each chosen to disrupt the viewers sense of the past. The capsules would routinely go viral, and it began to occur to me that there must be a reason for this. I decided to try to figure out what this reason was, and to see whether it was possible to codify my approach so that it could be applied to any collection of archive photographs. I wanted to reduce it down as much as possible to a simple formula. The result was S.P.E.E.D. Using the five letters of the formula, I could look at any old photograph and accurately predict whether it would engage with an audience. The higher a photograph's S.P.E.E.D. score, the more likely it would be a viral hit.[13]

Wild did not reveal what comprised the S.P.E.E.D. score nor how it was calculated. But clearly @Retronaut and @HistoryInPics shared a central logic: re-package elements of the past into discreet social media packages according to a prescribed formula, stimulate the user to action, induce virality and use the virality to drive the business model and gain influence. The intention of @HistoryInPics was always to make money. Di Petta and Cameron recognized that if they could garner millions of views on their content through virality, they could leverage the audience to generate revenue. In December 2014, they did just that. They received $2 million from investors and launched a company called All Day Media.[14] According to Crunchbase, the company was headquartered in Los Angeles, and described itself as "highly visual and shareable editorial content" for "mobile-first Millennial audiences … sharing stories with people who want to be amazed by the world."[15] The site did not last; today, AllDay.com no longer exists. But @HistoryInPics endured, eventually earning ten times as many Twitter followers as any professional historian. Virality was critical; the success of the business model depended on it.

Like other successful e-history, both accounts also promised their followers instant gratification. If offline history takes effort to penetrate, e-history is effortless to retrieve. If history content is lengthy and nuanced, e-history delivers quick and satisfying answers. Such was the case with @HistoryInPics. Its very origins were rooted in shortcuts to knowledge. Di Petta stated in his TEDx talk that at his home in rural Australia he dreamed of quitting school and moving to Los Angeles to become a celebrity. He particularly "hated" history class; as soon as his school allowed it, he dropped it. He and Kyle Cameron commiserated in their dislike of history class by sharing "cool, rare historical photos" between them: Frank Sinatra performing a tablecloth trick or Johnny Cash performing at Folsom Prison. The two friends launched @HistoryInPics to purposefully shun "long wordy textbooks." The title of his TEDxTeen Talk was, in fact, "How to learn history in 140 characters."[16] Di Petta's experience with @HistoryInPics taught him valuable lessons about the social Web that echoed the debates around Wikipedia a decade earlier: (1) "You no longer need to read 140 pages; you can read 140 characters"; (2) "You don't need expertise to be heard"; and (3) as far as history was concerned, "It was the method I didn't enjoy, not the content."[17]

@HistoryInPics deliberately positioned itself as an antidote to professional history—even as, like Timehop before it, the account used Abraham Lincoln as its avatar and borrowed from the terminology of history. The account was predicated on the notion that disrupters had stepped in where institutional history had fallen short. Its posts offered appealing content without the laborious and time-consuming aspects of history class or professional study. @HistoryInPics did not require much thought; users could simply enjoy the pretty pictures. Expertise was not required.

Similarly, Chris Wild's marketing of Retronaut invoked *e*-history's promise to deliver an instantly gratifying effect:

> Wild, a former museum archivist, has revolutionized the way we think of dusty photos, turning them into a sensation that has taken the Internet by surprise. He has selected over 300 of the best photographs from the site's most visited eras and themes, mashing up Victoriana with vintage advertising from the '60s and '70s and unearthing rare snapshots of evil dictators taking vacations. Page by page, this unconventional, thought-provoking photographic time machine will change what you think you know about history.[18]

Like Memolane before it, @Retronaut used the "time machine" metaphor to reinforce a notion of instantaneous travel back to the past. Similar to Timehop on Facebook or r/OldSchoolCool on Reddit, the goal of @Retronaut was to make the past feel familiar and relatable, to embrace the human-interest and to stir people's emotions. @HistoryInPics purported to rescue moments from the past that had been previously burdened by heavy texts or boring lectures. @Retronaut surfaced quirky and unusual photographs that had been buried out of sight in museums and archives. The history profession, they argued, had not unlocked the wonder and emotion of these images on the social Web, and these accounts filled the void. Both @HistoryInPics and @Retronaut suggested they'd rectified those shortcomings, rescuing the past from the clutches of history.

Why did any of this matter? Recall that Twitter began in 2006 as a status-update service; users told their friends what they were doing, thinking or feeling, for example, "waiting for a flight to Zurich and London" or "migraine while driving."[19] From its foundations, Twitter was a social network built on public displays of status. @HistoryInPics was, essentially, an extension of the Twitter status update; to unearth a surprising or evocative image from the past was an indicator of status. To continually make content go viral was an imprimatur of status. To surpass hundreds of thousands and, eventually, millions of followers conveyed status as a history communicator. This all occurred on a platform that was fast becoming the most influential social network in the world. At a time when the status of professional history was under threat, enrollments declining and public relevance in question, suddenly a new player had emerged who achieved coveted status in a very short period of time.

Scholars responded by criticizing @HistoryInPics with even more intensity than they had Wikipedia a decade earlier. Historians attacked the account for its lack of context, lack of critical assessment of the photographs, for playing to myths and for not adhering to a disciplinary methodology.[20] One historian wrote that @HistoryInPics was "bad for history, bad for Twitter, and bad for you."[21] But like Wikipedia, the success of @HistoryInPics was too compelling for journalists and the broader public to ignore. @HistoryInPics was not only profiled by *The Atlantic* but in newspapers in the United States, the United Kingdom, The Netherlands and Australia.[22] Its posts appeared in a daily column called "The Morning Brew" in *The Oklahoman* from 2016 to 2018. The account was cited by librarians as a cultural literacy resource.[23] Di Petta was hired as a consultant to Bustle, Yik Yak and the World Wildlife Fund. Virality had become correlated with credibility.

Historians argued that because @HistoryInPics had no intrinsic value as an accurate educational resource, it should not have been celebrated in the public eye. But within the ethos of the social Web, @HistoryInPics was not valuable for its own sake, but rather by virtue of the retweets, favorites, followers and media attention it garnered. It was *extrinsically valuable*, its worth derived from its ability to accumulate social capital, status and, essentially, move merchandise. Individuals who can manipulate the platforms get celebrated by the news media and Silicon Valley in the same manner as entrepreneurs and celebrities: for raising money and attracting attention. To paraphrase scholar Eugene McCarraher, the viral past possesses the same enchantment as other emblems of capitalistic success.[24] @HistoryInPics was a rags-to-riches tale, glamorized by media coverage that marveled at how two teenagers achieved Internet fame overnight. The viral past on Twitter was celebrated for its *attributes*, not its *veracity*.

At the same time @HistoryInPics and @Retronaut engineered virality to make elements of the past visible on our screens, other history accounts that were more rigorous and scholarly remained invisible. These included a New York History blog and Twitter account launched by a man named John Warren;[25] a blog and Twitter called the Ultimate History Blog;[26] the website and Twitter account Histocrats, launched by a group of independent history educators;[27] a History of Parliament blog and Twitter account launched in England;[28] a blog and Twitter account launched by an independent historian named Sean Unger; and an Appalachian history blog and Twitter account launched by an independent historian named Dave Tabler. There were also thousands of institutions worldwide—museums, libraries and archives—with Twitter accounts that featured historic photographs. But of interest to us are the independent accounts because they are truer apples-to-apples comparison with @Retronaut and @HistoryInPics. They, too, were independent voices who sought to leverage the social Web to supplement or, perhaps, disrupt traditional history. These accounts had some success; a few reached several thousand Twitter followers. But none achieved the visibility and virality of @HistoryInPics. Despite being led by history professionals and history teachers—or perhaps because of it—these *e*-history accounts never made the past go viral. Their content may have circulated within like-minded clusters of history educators, but did not spread to other clusters with any speed or intensity. The projects became by historians, for historians (or other history enthusiasts). The accounts may have had *intrinsic* value due to their accuracy and veracity. Yet, they went almost completely unnoticed on Twitter. Virality meant that some pasts would be omnipresent on our screens, while others would never reach us. That outcome had nothing to do with the importance or accuracy of the information.

The consequences of a media ecosystem that endowed viral content on Twitter with significance, authority, credibility and newsworthiness have been well-documented. No starker illustration existed than the rise of candidate-turned-president Donald Trump, whose purposefully inflammatory tweets starting in 2011 were intended to stoke attention and outrage. Trump picked fights with comedian Rosie O'Donnell, launched diatribes against China and Iran, and subscribed to conspiracy theories about global warming and President Obama's birth certificate.[29] His tweets were designed to go viral, to be controversial and to attract media coverage and provoke responses from clusters of outraged Conservatives. It worked. Trump's 89.5 million likes and retweets dwarfed Hillary Clinton's 41.6 million during the 2016 U.S. presidential campaign.[30] And just as @HistoryInPics attracted media attention for its viral rise, Trump attracted inordinate media coverage for his. Trump earned more media coverage via social media than any other Republican candidate and Secretary Clinton by wide margins. By the time of the election, Trump had earned $4.96 billion of ad-equivalent coverage, while Clinton had earned $3.24 billion.[31]

In response to the candidacy and election of Trump in 2015 and 2016, new like-minded clusters emerged on Twitter that sought to resist Donald

Trump and his brand of Conservative politics. These like-minded clusters included professional historians, journalists, media pundits and Progressive activists. Today's historians are committed to making historical narratives less male, less white, less Eurocentric and more advancing of social justice causes. Historians seek to graduate students who will challenge unjust and corrupt power structures, actively pursue justice for victims, and display acute sensitivity to race, class and gender.[32] For historians, President Trump represented opposition to all of that: a white, rich, corporate patriarch with little sensitivity to race, class or gender. Trump's ascendancy to the top of the Republican Party encapsulated all that was perilous about American conservatism. Even before his election, Trump's brand of politics was cited by historians as one of four "significant problems" facing the profession.[33]

In the wake of Trump's election, Twitter became a primary online meeting ground for like-minded Progressives to speak out against the president and his worldview. The year 2016 saw the highest percentage of historians join Twitter, followed closely by 2017.[34] Historian Seth Cotlar, for example, stated that he began tweeting during the 2016 primaries and tweeted in full-on crisis mode the morning after election day.[35] Another historian said he began to speak out online in 2017 explicitly to "reject the racist candidacy and policies of Donald Trump."[36] During the Trump presidency, Twitter became more politically Left than the U.S. population, with historians indicative of the average user. The average Twitter user was more educated, more likely to identify as a Democrat, more sympathetic to social justice causes and likely to earn more than the average U.S. citizen.[37] Like-minded clusters across the platform became linked by an overarching cause: opposing the 45th president and the system they felt made him possible.

Within these clusters of users newly connected by a common cause, professional historians on Twitter (a.k.a. "Twitterstorians") began to go viral. Professional historians benefited from the same mechanisms that @HistoryInPics and Donald Trump had, and which they had criticized only a few years earlier. Tweets by professional historians that confronted Trump or Conservative pundits provoked rapid sharing within like-minded clusters in short periods of time. The decisions by Twitter users to retweet were based on *social* factors, not educational ones. Professional *e*-history went viral because the tweets resonated with *other users* within the anti-Trump #Resistance. As a result, during the years 2015–2020 professional history began to feel much more relevant.

The foremost example was Kevin Kruse, a professor of history at Princeton University and a scholar of American conservatism, voter suppression, Civil Rights and urban/suburban politics. Kruse became famous on Twitter in the same manner that Trump had—by picking fights. Kruse used Twitter to refute Conservative pundits and ideologues, most notably Charlie Kirk (a co-founder of Turning Point USA) and Dinesh D'Souza, a frequent contributor to PragerU. Kruse used punchy Twitter threads to argue against D'Souza's interpretations of history. The insults back-and-forth became symbolic of the broader culture wars between those who endorsed Trump's worldview and those who opposed it.

Activists and academics gravitated toward the Kruse-D'Souza conflict and retweeted it. The Twitter algorithm picked up the attention signals and raised the visibility in more people's feeds. Journalists took notice and wrote profiles of Kruse deeming him history's "attack dog."[38] The novelty of an Ivy League professor dunking on a Conservative pundit made for a compelling story. In other words, *the attributes of the conflict made it go viral*, not its substance. Were a historian to have published the same rebuttals to D'Souza in a journal article, it would not have had the same resonance (and, indeed, numerous historians have done so). The culture wars playing out over social media lent it visibility and salience during a period of intensely fierce political battles being litigated online.

Such Twitter threads by Kruse and others were still the viral past, only a new incarnation. The tweets were discrete media products that packaged an element (or elements) of the past for consumption on the social Web, and which attempted to leverage the mechanisms of the social Web in order to gain visibility. But they were now strategically created by professional historians, as opposed to amateurs. The effect was the same: virality led to more opportunities and fame for Kruse, as well as more status. By the close of the Trump Presidency, Kruse had amassed 450,000 followers, more than other professional historians on the platform (though still only 10 percent of @HistoryInPics).

Just as accounts had imitated @HistoryInPics, professional historians imitated Kruse. Historian Heather Cox Richardson tweeted about the Republican Party's politics of exclusion in response to the Justice Brett Kavanaugh hearings. Historians Joshua Rothman and Beth Lew-Williams used family separation among enslaved populations to argue against Trump's family separation policies at the U.S.-Mexico border. Once again, the news media gravitated to the confrontations. The same writer who had condemned @HistoryInPics four years earlier wrote a column for Slate in

2018 that praised professional historians for effectively exploiting Twitter, the headline being "Making History Go Viral."[39] (It should be noted that we have no evidence whether the Twitter threads were actually viral—i.e., followed a sigmoid curve pattern—or were simply seen by a large number of people. That would make for an interesting future history communication study.) The same mechanics that had been dangerous in the hands of the amateur were lauded in the hands of the professionals. Suddenly, during the Trump Presidency, professional history felt more urgent as more historians leveraged Twitter's algorithm and like-minded user base. That their viral tweets sparked reactions among Progressives on Twitter lent them extrinsic value to the overarching cause of defeating Trump.

Two final points are necessary to conclude this analysis. The first is the importance of media logic to virality, particularly on Twitter. Journalists have an outsized presence on the platform; at various points in time, 83 percent of journalists used Twitter and journalists represented 25 percent of Twitter's verified users.[40] Journalists and news producers possess certain assumptions about what information is worthy of public attention. Longtime political journalist David Broder once observed that "the press in all its forms is episodic" and that "reporters are instinctively fight promoters."[41] The world operating as it should is not particularly newsworthy, but a conflict or a disruption of the established order is. Information that is novel, discrepant and immediate makes people take notice.[42] Andrew Chadwick and other scholars have characterized this as "media logic."[43]

Chadwick argues that a certain media logic undergirds the hybrid communications system we operate in, comprising social media, broadcast media, print media and in-person events. In other words, what makes for a good news story defines what we deem to be publicly valued information.[44] Those wishing to influence public discourse must adapt to fit such media logic. Chadwick also writes that media logic shapes what the public expects politics to be.[45] As the viral past became embedded within the politics of Twitter, I would argue that media logic also came to shape what the public expected *history* to be. In other words, the *e*-history on Twitter that was deemed publicly valuable information shared the characteristics of what made for a compelling news story: novel, discrepant, emotional, episodic and with conflict at its core. The news media especially crave symbols that visibly convey drama as it unfolds.[46] Twitter arguments between Liberal academics and Conservative pundits offered journalists consistent symbolic, unfolding drama. The histories that symbolized broader political and cultural fights became publicly valued, online and offline. The histories that lacked that resonance became buried in the feed.

This leads to a final point, namely, the pasts that did *not* get seen on Twitter during the period of Kevin Kruse, Heather Cox Richardson and others. Hundreds of professional historians tweeted throughout the Trump administration on subjects beyond the presidency or the American culture wars, on topics such as German history, histories of the Ottoman Empire, Chinese history, histories of African nations and Australian histories. That *e*-history was far less visible in our feeds in the United States. It did not conform to prevailing media logic. It may have had *intrinsic* value to its practitioners, but it did not go viral because it did not signify the broader culture wars and did not make for a good news story. It had no *extrinsic* value—which is what ultimately matters on the social Web, and increasingly, beyond it.

Like the PragerU video about the Civil War, tweets by Kevin Kruse, Heather Cox Richardson and others went viral not solely because they communicated accurate history—thousands of professional historians did that each day. The tweets said something about other users within like-minded clusters, namely, that they were part of the anti-Trump #Resistance in a predominantly Progressive Twitterverse. Much like the PragerU video, the symbolism as part of the culture wars played a crucial role in bringing it to attention. Twitter played a significant role in determining which pasts were deemed publicly valuable and which were not. Twitter also helped to dictate *who* became a publicly celebrated history communicator and who did not. The viral past elevated the careers of @HistoryInPics, Kevin Kruse, Heather Cox Richardson and others whose brand of *e*-history conformed to a certain set of conditions.

The addition of the viral past into the *e*-history universe had one further consequence: the further flattening of *e*-history into a competing war of online symbols. As the political debates of the 2010s raged on, *e*-history became a potent weapon in broader political conflicts that could be deployed to score political points or win political arguments. As the speed of online discourse increased, the social Web became a competing marketplace of fast-moving symbols. In any given online debate, *e*-history could be lobbed at the opposing side to win an argument or re-frame a debate. *e*-history proved to be an extremely effective weapon for scholars and activists. It would also, as we'll see in the next chapter, be a potent weapon for foreign disinformation agents seeking to sow chaos and discord within American society.

Amid all this, Twitter's growth actually began to stall in the mid-2010s. In its place surged Instagram, surpassing 500 million users in 2016.[47] As an app that privileged the iconic image above all else, the *e*-history universe that had been flooded with the viral past would now add the visual past. These visual pasts would become prolific and potent symbols that could be exploited by actors with both honest intentions and nefarious ones.

CHAPTER 6

The Visual Past

In spring 2015, venture capitalist Mary Meeker published her annual slide presentation about the state of the social Web.[1] One slide asked what teenagers felt was their most important social network. The answer was Instagram. Launched in 2010, Instagram had been gaining in popularity among teens while Twitter and Facebook were gradually becoming less relevant to them. By September 2015, the platform surpassed 400 million users.[2] By the end of 2020, it had more than 1 billion accounts.[3] Already by 2018, 90 percent of Instagram users were under the age of 35 and 85 percent of teenagers used Instagram at least once per month.[4] While professional historians were on Twitter refuting @HistoryInPics and Donald Trump, the visual past was expanding on Instagram reaching the eyes of millions of teens, students and millennials.

One such account was History Cool Kids, launched in January 2016 by Dain Lee. Five years later, it had more than 1.4 million followers.[5] Building on the premise of @HistoryInPics, History Cool Kids posted nostalgic photographs from the past that relied on emotion and human interest to grab attention. Its images included a black marshal who may have inspired the Lone Ranger, a Union soldier from Rhode Island who died during the Civil War, and a Chinese diplomat during World War II who helped to save European Jews. Unlike @HistoryInPics, History Cool Kids included detailed captions—often several hundred words long—and a URL for more information. The sources for the captions ranged from media

© The Author(s), under exclusive license to Springer Nature Switzerland AG 2022
J. Steinhauer, *History, Disrupted*,
https://doi.org/10.1007/978-3-030-85117-0_6

companies like HISTORY.com, NPR, The Conversation and Owlcation to the websites of Yad Vashem, the Uffizi and the Wellcome Library.

Unlike Xavier Di Petta and Kyle Cameron, Dain Lee professed to love history. He started History Cool Kids because he wanted to share "all the cool stories" he "didn't learn in history class"—repeating a common refrain of *e*-history as an antidote to scholastic history.[6] He wanted to create a learning experience for his peers that was fun (echoing Ward Cunningham and Jimmy Wales), and the opposite of how students thought of history education. "It saddens me when people think history is boring," Lee told the online magazine Whalebone in 2019.[7] Indeed, the photographer who interviewed Lee in Whalebone remarked that Lee made the "oft-hated school subject" of history cool again. "When you think of history class, you may be transported back to squirming uncomfortably in your high school desk chair listening to your history teacher droning through a PowerPoint," she wrote. "Or maybe you are reminded of that 3,000-page textbook … you had to lug back and forth from home to class. Scrolling through History Cool Kids is nothing like that."[8] Like @HistoryInPics, History Cool Kids shunned "long wordy textbooks" for "cool, rare historical photos." If offline history is stodgy, *e*-history is stimulating; if offline history is didactic, *e*-history is tinged with emotion and human interest.

The sensibility of History Cool Kids resonated with Instagram users. Elle Magazine praised the account for its touching stories and "side of pop culture cool."[9] The website Gramlist, which scours Instagram for influential accounts, lauded History Cool Kids for being full of "pictures of people you want to hang out with" and added that "what really draws you in is the style and the attitude."[10] The writer for Whalebone remarked that History Cool Kids allowed users to "upgrade the mix of food porn and beautiful places you can't afford to go to and beautiful people you'll probably never meet with some history."[11] A journalist I spoke with who followed History Cool Kids loved how she felt like she was discovering the past alongside Lee. "Instagram is a good platform for scrolling, looking at friends' babies, and then I also get History Cool Kids," she added. "I never thought about history visually."[12]

History Cool Kids was one of the thousands of *e*-history accounts that took the discipline of history—predicated on books, articles and lectures—and transposed it to Instagram. If Wikipedia placed the amateur on par with the expert, and Facebook and Twitter elevated nostalgic imagery in our feeds, the visual past accelerated *e*-history's agenda-advancing and reality-suggesting functions through curated and filtered progressions of images. The visual past promised the user that complex events and histories that could be condensed and represented in iconic and symbolic forms,[13] a "good-enough" historical understanding wrapped in a visually arresting package.

Distinct from the viral past—which can be textual or visual and which purposefully aspires to contagion—the visual past filters the historical record in eye-catching ways in order to stop us (at least momentarily) from scrolling. It is a byproduct of platforms such as Instagram designed from their inception not to send content virally through networks, but to filter and beautify photographs in the most reaction-inducing manner, imbuing them with greater significance in the process.[14] For these reasons, the visual past on Instagram taps into battles over how "history" and "the past" become iconized on social media—as well as how e-history increasingly throughout the 2010s became a series of icons and symbols, deployed on a fast-moving social Web in order to advance agendas and frame reality.

Web users may not realize how much e-history exists on Instagram. One search for #history on the app found more than 24 million posts. Popular hashtags included #historychannel (180K posts), #historymemes (123K posts), #historygeek (84.7K posts), #historyfacts (43.5K posts) and #historymeme (18.8K posts). Accounts succeeded for the same reasons that e-history succeeded on other platforms: user-centric, commercially viable, instantly gratifying and extrinsically valuable. But perhaps more than anywhere else, Instagram privileged the attributes of e-history more than its contents. The iconic resonance of an image on Instagram was crucial to it becoming visible in our feeds. Instagram was not only a social network, but a broadcasting network powered by an image economy. From its earliest days, Instagram was described as a "stream of postcards, shot by phone."[15] Scholars have written how postcards are carriers of cultural values;[16] as such, each Instagram post embodied and expressed a set of values to younger audiences. For these reasons, the platform was almost immediately exploited by companies and brands to broadcast their values to a new generation of consumers. An array of aspirational emotions came to underpin this brand-driven digital capitalism: beauty, desire, lust, glory, valor, excitement, entertainment, intrigue, wonder and longing. These fantastical desires were encapsulated in the Whalebone writer's references to "food porn," "beautiful places you can't afford to go to" and "beautiful people you'll probably never meet." Since being acquired by Facebook in 2012, the Instagram algorithm has been continually optimized to keep audiences engaged in this image-driven economy, viewing ads, buying and selling products, and interacting with attractive influencers who signified an aspirational lifestyle.[17]

Teenagers overwhelmingly preferred that brands contacted them on Instagram than other social platforms, and corporations took notice.[18] Brands on Instagram saw a 115 percent increase in organic reach from 2012 to 2017, while 68 percent of users engaged with brands regularly on the platform.[19] Corporations spent $1.07 billion on influencer marketing on Instagram in 2017,[20] and Instagram influencing became so lucrative that the Federal Trade Commission stepped in to regulate it.[21] Whereas Facebook forged connections around views and beliefs, Instagram forged connections around attributes and aesthetics. The attributes of the person or product were being marketed as much as anything else: Carefree. Adventurous. Elegant. Committed. Performance-driven. Passionate. Attractive. Fit. Wealthy. Beautiful. Righteous. Successful and so on. On Instagram, young people could quickly see whether the attributes of a person or product aligned with what they perceived their values and attributes to be—or what they aspired their attributes and values to be. Using iconic imagery to stimulate longing, desire and aspiration could allow actors to manipulate content into our feeds, including e-history.

The e-history that was iconic, aspirational, beautiful or arresting was, thus, better aligned with Instagram culture. History Cool Kids owed its visibility, in part, to its branding as "cool" and its target demographics of "kids." In 2018, Korean researchers examined the appeal of Instagram and found that youth used the platform as a source of information about what their peers were up to: what clothes they wore, what exercises they performed, where they traveled, what unique experiences they had and who they hung out with.[22] Thousands of celebrities forged careers using their good looks, charm, personality and lifestyle to become the cool kids that other users wanted to be friends with. Indeed, that was how they were dubbed by media outlets. Instagram celebrities such as Luka Sabbat were described as the "cool kid at the party we all want to be."[23] These influencers exhibited a beautiful sense of style; traveled to exotic locations; and presented to their followers an attractive, friendly face that, over time, forged an emotional connection. In one way or another, these influencers strategically presented—and represented—an aspirational lifestyle that was unique, compelling and highly visual.[24] Instagram showed its users the "cool kids" of today; History Cool Kids showed them the "cool kids" of yesterday.

These aspirational qualities directly affected other historical content and history communicators who gained visibility on Instagram. War photography constituted one such example, a sub-genre of the visual past that provided few documentary details about the scenes it represented but that offered visually arresting images that functioned as "emblematic signifiers."[25] In other words, these Instagram feeds reduced hugely complex and destructive events into a series of iconic photographs that espoused a set of aspirational attributes: heroism, patriotism, courage, sacrifice, etc. Many such war-themed Instagram feeds ranked among the *e*-history accounts with the largest followings—some with hundreds of thousands of followers—depicting iconic and visually arresting imagery from conflicts such as World War I and World War II. Some accounts posted black and white photographs; others colorized the images (colorized photos are, in themselves, another sub-genre of the visual past that seek to stop us from scrolling to admire the vivid visuals). The iconic imagery of war did well on Instagram precisely because it offered a curated selection of the past that captured aspirational values—not to mention glorified versions of masculinity.

More broadly, the #history posts on Instagram were often photographs of iconic historical figures such as John F. Kennedy, Winston Churchill, President Obama, Queen Elizabeth and Michael Jackson, along with iconic artifacts such as churches, archaeological ruins, paintings, statues and famous posters. There were innumerable Instagram accounts that trafficked in these "postcards" from the past, some run by history institutions and others by non-historians. But they all relied on a selection of iconic images to, in the words of scholar Leigh Raiford, "distill and symbolize a range of complex events, ideas, and ideologies" into exemplary forms.[26]

By being predicated on the iconic image, Instagram privileged aspects of the past that were heavily documented by photography, as opposed to centuries prior when photography did not exist. It privileged celebrities and world leaders who spent their lives in the public eye and for whom many professional photographs existed. And it privileged events (such as wars) and social movements (such as Civil Rights) for which thousands of photographs were purposefully and strategically taken. The photographs from the nineteenth through the twenty-first centuries that possessed iconographic and memorializing attributes, thus, became omnipresent in the feed and over-represented as "history" for Instagram users. Prior centuries (e.g., the seventeenth century) and less symbolic conflicts (e.g., the

Persian Gulf War) were largely invisible. Hundreds of Instagram accounts, for example, were dedicated to World War II, while none were dedicated to the Hundred Years' War (1337–1453) or the Moamoria Rebellion (1769–1806). There simply weren't enough visual assets from these conflicts available on the Web to produce viable business models, nor had these conflicts been elevated (by governments, journalists, activists or other political actors) to iconographic status.

e-history on Instagram has also skewed American or Eurocentric, that is, parts of the world where digitized and accessible photo archives existed that could be quickly repurposed. For regions of the world where photo archives were restricted, destroyed or non-existent, the visual past simply could not thrive in the same manner. Among World War II accounts, most Instagram feeds did not stray far from the European and Pacific Theaters of Operation, rendering the histories of the conflicts in North Africa, China-Burma-India and the Aleutian Islands nearly invisible. Like the "Snowzilla" Wikipedia entry, the curators of these accounts chose source materials that were the most easily accessible, privileging certain archives and disadvantaging others. That, then, got broadcast to 1 billion users, predominantly younger people, suggesting an exhaustive or definitive record of the past when it was, in fact, barely a sliver. One set of pasts became visible; other pasts became invisible. The result was not indicative of significance or accuracy, but rather a reflection of the platform's designs and the retrievability of certain archives. The ability to quickly surface and repurpose imagery that was already imbued with iconic characteristics dictated the business model of how to succeed on Instagram. That had no correlation with rigor, significance or editorial discernment.

Though Instagram had triple the number of users as Twitter, not as many scholars used the platform to communicate history professionally. (Though many used Instagram for personal reasons.) To be an effective history communicator on Instagram as an individual, one would have to turn oneself into an icon. One would have to post images that convey a set of aspirational values while engaging in aspirational activities. One would have to be a History Cool Kid, someone that young Instagram users aspire to be, experiencing things young Instagrammers aspire to experience. Instagram users may aspire to be a celebrity eating exotic foods and traveling around the world.[27] They may be less inclined to aspire to teach two to four courses per week and spend the remaining hours in committee meetings, grading papers and conducting solitary research in the archives. As one Harvard professor put it crudely, "few people are interested in how professors spend their time."²⁸ But Instagram users might follow such a person if there was a visually compelling way to suggest such a reality. What would it look like for a historian to use Instagram in this way? Such a case study exists from the sciences in the person of Science Sam.

Science Sam is a Science Communicator who has amassed more than 100,000 followers on Instagram. She has used the medium in the manner that successful Instagram influencers do: aspirational photographs where she is at the center of the action, hiking atop mountains, traveling to conferences and in the lab with enthusiastic colleagues. Along the way, she has touted the value of scientific inquiry and shared highlights from her research. She has successfully turned herself into an icon. For her usage of Instagram, Science Sam was criticized by a fellow female scientist named Meghan Wright in the pages of *Science* magazine. Wright wrote, "Publicly documenting the cute outfit I wear and the sweet smile I brandish in the lab isn't going to help me build a fulfilling career in a field where women hold less senior positions, are paid less, and are continuously underrated. Time spent on Instagram is time away from research, and this affects women in science more than men. That's unfair. Let's not celebrate that."²⁹

Science Sam leaned into the tropes of Instagram in order to lift up women in science. Yet, some academics saw it as demeaning. One of Science Sam's posts featured her at Comic-Con. Contrast that with historian Jill Lepore, a professor of American history at Harvard University and one of America's preeminent intellectuals. In an interview with the *Chronicle of Higher Education* in 2018, Lepore criticized an attempt by the Chronicle to depict her as Wonder Woman in an article about her book on the iconic superhero. "When my Wonder Woman book came out, The Chronicle of Higher Education published a cartoon of me as Wonder Woman. I was appalled," Lepore said. "It was an incredible trivialization of a female academic who writes serious intellectual and political history to depict me dressed as a character I had identified as coming from the visual culture of pornography."³⁰ For the *Chronicle*, the Jill Lepore-as-Wonder Woman image was likely intended to depict Lepore as an iconic hero of history. To Lepore, it was an insult that pandered to misogynistic stereotypes about women—articulated in much the same tone as Meghan Wright criticized Science Sam.

These exchanges reflected deeper fault lines over how representations of women online and off can become disrespectful and trivializing. The history of science blog, "Lady Science," wrote a missive on its website in

2019 about how its editors were abandoning the American Historical Association annual meeting because of how feminist scholars were treated by their male peers.[31] Such exchanges stake out battle lines over the "brand identities" of professions such as history and science as they get increasingly commodified in visual-first media. Debates over how women scholars get depicted, and depict themselves, on a platform such as Instagram are part of larger debates about how women are represented in fields that have traditionally been male-dominated and continue to face challenges of sexual assault and sexual harassment. Becoming an icon on social media risks reinforcing gender roles and hegemonic messaging, elevating women whose appearance conforms to conventional standards of beauty while disadvantaging women of different races, ages, abilities and body types.

Science Sam leaned into the tropes and conventions of Instagram to connect with an audience visually. By posting content that Instagram culture rewarded, she achieved visibility that, in turn, she hoped would hoist up women in science and scientific inquiry in general. She engaged an audience in learning that otherwise may not have been prone to do so. Her detractors felt that she was embracing the very inequities that female scientists should be working to overturn. In her interview, Lepore essentially laid out a similar dilemma for professional historians: embrace popular culture, app culture, corporate media and social media's hegemonic sensibilities (especially on Instagram)—or criticize such tropes and work to dismantle them. To embrace history as a commodity on Instagram in exchange for visibility and influence, or not? To lean into popular culture and app culture—or to stand outside it, criticizing it and dissecting it from afar? A visual past on Instagram that necessitated iconography, brand identity and aspirational attributes in order to gain visibility becomes as contested a battleground as Twitter, Facebook or Wikipedia.

As the image economy became more powerful throughout the 2010s, social media became flooded with iconographic imagery from the past, appropriated and re-appropriated into different contexts in order to advance agendas or re-frame debates. The visual past was frequently deployed by activists and journalists in ways that purported to offer simplicity and moral clarity on current events. *e*-history promises to provide instantly gratifying results and clear and easy answers. Time-consuming scholarship and critical thinking are replaced in favor of the "satisficing" effect, a good-enough understanding of history that permits a user to participate in whatever debate may currently be ongoing. The social Web's ability to reward users who could instantly resurface and repurpose iconic imagery in any context turned out to have consequences, not solely for politics but also for misinformation and disinformation campaigns.

This was particularly true of Civil Rights photography, which in the 2010s was repeatedly appropriated and re-appropriated online as a means to build or reinforce a moral position, act as a sign of protest and win political arguments.[32] Much Civil Rights photography was strategically documented by activists during the 1950s and 1960s in order to sway public opinion and publicize violent acts against protestors.[33] But on the social Web, the rush to deploy memes and iconic imagery from Civil Rights in order to win fast-moving political debates in the present became fertile ground for foreign disinformation agents to sow discord, particularly on the issue of race in America. The visual past proved to be a potent weapon in the fight for public opinion online, used by activists and foreign disinformation agents alike.

The social media frenzy surrounding an encounter in Washington, D.C., on Martin Luther King, Jr., weekend in January 2019 provides one such case study. The uproar began the evening of Friday, January 18, 2019, when Twitter user @2020Fight posted a short video of a white teenager in a red Make America Great Again hat smirking at a Native American elder on the steps of the Lincoln Memorial. The white student had been in Washington, D.C., for the annual March for Life anti-abortion rally. The Native American man (who was also a Marine Corps veteran) had been participating in the Indigenous Peoples March that same weekend. Washington was in the midst of a partial government shutdown, wherein President Trump refused to sign any bills to open the federal government unless they included funds for a wall on the southern border of the United States. The entire scene unfolded on the steps of the Lincoln Memorial on Martin Luther King, Jr., weekend. An array of complex symbols was, thus, on display: activists, protestors, Native Americans, white Americans, senior citizens, teenagers, veterans and the specter of Martin Luther King, Abraham Lincoln, President Trump and political dysfunction looming over it all.

An edited video of the encounter was posted to Instagram and then shared on Reddit. The Twitter account @2020Fight, which purported to be a Progressive activist from California, then tweeted a very short segment of the video.[34] The account had more than 41,000 followers at the time, among them Progressive activists who had spent the past two years resisting the Trump administration. The @2020Fight tweet included the incendiary caption, "This MAGA loser gleefully bothering a Native American protestor at the Indigenous People's March."[35] It was a caption and video intentionally crafted to go viral, and that's precisely what occurred.

Following the sigmoid pattern described in our previous chapter, Progressive activists on Twitter immediately responded to @2020Fight with retweets and replies, circulating the imagery and caption within their like-minded clusters. That virality triggered the Twitter algorithm to surface the content to more users, bringing it to the attention of journalists, who quickly wrote breaking news stories that sent the video around the world. Within 24 hours, the video and caption purposefully designed to go viral had sparked a national and international media frenzy.[36]

During that frenzy, the visual past became a powerful weapon of activists, journalists and disinformation agents to frame the confrontation as an allegory for the broader condition of the United States. Framing such a confrontation quickly is important, as the original framing is usually the one that sticks.[37] Accounts with hashtags such as #votebluenomatterwho and #ImpeachtheMF,[38] as well as feminists, LGBT advocates and others involved with Progressive causes[39]—some actual people and some foreign agents—used the visual past to argue that the teenager in the video signified the racism and arrogance of white America, and, by proxy President Trump. Iconic imagery from the Civil Rights movement and World War II was hastily deployed in service of that narrative, intended to provide simplicity and moral clarity to an encounter that was, in reality, far more nuanced.[40] The memes and iconic images, communicated in rapid succession, delivered a satisfying and re-affirming jolt of emotion and solidarity to like-minded activists. They were valuable for their attributes, useful for their ability to suggest a reality, their visually arresting and attention-grabbing capabilities, and their capacity to signify the moral superiority of one side of the culture wars.

One Twitter user, @Harry_Callahan, replied to @2020Fight's tweet with a historical meme of an iconic lynching photograph. The image showed white men surrounding the charred body of William Brown after a horrific lynching in Omaha Nebraska in 1919. The text read in bold white letters: "Those 'Men' in the Background, They Did Not Go Away! They Had Children!!"[41] @Harry_Callahan purported to be a Progressive activist, though his true identity is unclear. At the time of his tweet, he had the hashtags #KremlinDon #PutinsLittleBitch and #Resist in his bio. The meme he tweeted had actually been created two years earlier, posted on imgrum.net as well as on a Pinterest board called Pseudo Science.[42] The original photograph had circulated on the Web since 2007, uploaded to the scholarly website BlackPast.org.[43] It had been added to Wikipedia in summer 2007;[44] circulated within racist and conspiratorial websites during President Obama's administration (including in Russian forums); and further circulated on Reddit, Wikipedia and 4chan during the Trump administration.[45] The image had been repurposed so often so as to become a "visual cliché,"[46] representing history without analyzing or explaining it. It had become valuable for its capacity to elicit an emotional response and to be repurposed into memes in order to advance political agendas. @Harry_Callahan deployed this visually arresting historical meme—either earnestly or deceptively—as part of a broader effort to use the visual past to win a political argument in the present by drawing a parallel to a past event.

Additional Civil Rights photography soon emerged online for the same purposes, lifted from existing corners of the e-history universe to be deployed in a fast-moving political fight. An adjunct professor of copyright law living in New Mexico, Barbara Waxer, replied to @2020Fight with a famous photograph of white youth harassing three Civil Rights activists during a lunch counter sit-in in Jackson, Mississippi, on May 28, 1963.[47] Waxer's tweet read, "Their history speaks for itself. A direct line in disrespect, arrogance and bigotry." The tweet was retweeted nearly 3000 times and favorited more than 15,000 times.[48] She later explained in a LinkedIn post that upon seeing the @2020Fight video late on Friday (her time), she "responded by drawing historical parallels."[49] Waxer was a specialist in finding free-to-use images on the Web that could be repurposed.[50] The iconic photograph she chose—taken by local newspaper photographer Fred Blackwell after he received advanced notice from the local NAACP about the sit-in—had circulated on the Web since at least 2008.[51] It had attained its symbolic status through its perpetual branding as an "iconic moment," including on the companion website for the book *We Shall Not Be Moved* in 2013;[52] on a website called Iconic Photos in 2015;[53] and in online newspapers such as the *Jackson Free Press* and *Los Angeles Times*.[54] The same photograph had been used by journalists four years earlier as another "historic parallel" to an image of a drowned Syrian refugee,[55] and one year earlier as a parallel to two black men being removed from a Starbucks.[56] Thus, as scholar Lene Hansen has written, the iconic image is presented as if its message is self-evident yet, "we find competing constructions of what that self-evident message is."[57]

By the next morning, the lunch counter photograph was ubiquitous on social media. A user named @mikeplugh tweeted that he had seen Waxer's reply to @2020Fight and therefore retweeted the sit-in photograph juxtaposed with a screenshot from the Lincoln Memorial event.[58] A reporter from the *Huffington Post*, tweeted the same juxtaposition.[59] A career coach named Lady Diana M, whose bio included the #impeachtrump hashtag, tweeted the same historical meme.[60] So did Twitter user @commishbob.[61] A Twitter user with the words "True Blue" in their bio tweeted an iconic photograph of Hazel Bryan, a white student, taunting a black teenager, Elizabeth Eckford, as Eckford and her classmates attempted to integrate an Arkansas public school in 1957.[62] That account was later suspended, likely a foreign influence agent. A user named Drucilla tweeted a photograph of a white power rally.[63] A user named To What End, replying to @2020Fight and the account @lulu_says2 (both suspended for being foreign influence accounts) tweeted a photograph of white teenagers surrounding a black man at a lunch counter.[64] Other Twitter users—some real activists and some foreign influence accounts—posted photographs of Nazi youth.[65] Progressive activists, aided and inflamed by foreign agents, used the visual past to make the argument that a high school student in Kentucky was the direct descendant of lynch mobs, Jim Crow segregationists and Nazis within a frenetic 24-hour period that had little to do with history but everything to do with instantly gratifying, emblematic images that condensed complex historical phenomena into digestible social media products aimed at advancing a political agenda.

A few days following the incident, Twitter suspended @2020Fight. The account had used a false headshot and had tweeted hundreds of times per day.[66] Though the account claimed to belong to a Progressive school teacher in California,[67] it had links to a website that argued teachers should carry firearms in schools.[68] The accounts that shared the video from Instagram to Reddit were also suspicious. The video was posted into the sub-Reddit r/PoliticalVideos by u/ARREST_HILLARY_NOW.[69] It was posted into r/trashy by a since-deleted accounted, and re-posted by a user named u/MaDdBlaKkNews.[70] It was also posted into r/Fuckthealtright.[71] It's unlikely the students who initially recorded the incident owned multiple Reddit accounts on both sides of the political aisle. A malicious actor had intentionally posted the video into various sub-Reddits with different headlines, trying to determine which would spark the fiercest emotional response. Once the most provocative combination had been achieved, it was shared on Twitter. A global media frenzy had been instigated by simple A/B testing by foreign agents.

Meanwhile on Instagram, foreign influence accounts intermixed with activists and Instagram users to continue to inflame the debate:

- timscott5613: "Aren't they taught in school that the Native Americans are the original Americans"
- jamessmithitis: "The Powhatan grabbed any tools or weapons available and killed all English settlers they found, including men, women, and children of all ages. Chief Opechancanough led a coordinated series of surprise attacks by the Powhatan Confederacy that killed 347 people, a quarter of the English population of the Virginia colony."[72]
- faye.westman: "@realandrewsessor your not even an Adult yet, neither am I but please don't come on her clearly defending someone who is smiling at a Native American practicing his religion and culture. I'm only 12 years old and I know that the Native American were driven out of THEIR land. It is a disgrace that white southerners think they had the right of taking land from people who have been here for thousands of generations. I live in Minnesota and there was natives driven out of my state to. It is horrible of what has become. I do indeed love America and what we have, and where we are. But how we got America to be, how it is today is not okay. The actions were not okay. With respect."
- the_good_news_: "@freegranny6 You say 'native american' as if they were one unified people living in peace and harmony. That's pure fantasy. Native American tribes fought each other and took each other's resources for hundreds of years before the first European every stepped foot. In 1873, the Souix tribe massacred 75–100 Pawnee, mostly women and children, mutilating them and even burning them alive. This isnt to say natives were more violent than Europeans. I'm simply saying that the native Americans were not all peaceful people, most tribes had warfare."
- poision22romance: "These are the descendants of the alleged 4 fathers of this disrespectful country. Expell all of them. Much respect to my elder that stood his ground ♥♥ and show who was the ignorant one."
- wolf_in_the_wilderness: "@millikenrenee the romance of the natives? Give me a break. They were massacred, raped, their land forceably

taken from them, their culture destroyed by forcing them to convert to a foreign religion and their children taken from them. In all seriousness, who wouldn't have problems after that? Learn some history, gain some empathy."
- cyfilmproductions: "These kids need to be educated about their ancestors past deeds."

The first two accounts ceased to exist shortly after the social media frenzy had died down, likely foreign agents. Foreign agents had used video, visuals, memes, Instagram, Reddit and Twitter to turn a fraught encounter in Washington, D.C., into a visually and racially charged social media frenzy with international ramifications. Within this frenzy, Web users within the ecosystem—including disinformation agents, journalists and activists—grabbed the most iconic and arresting imagery available and deployed it quickly within a highly visual and symbolic information environment, for the purposes of stoking reactions and framing a narrative. The visual past detached from its context ceases to be about the past at all; it becomes an effective way to weaponize arguments about the present.

The 2019 incident was similar in design to tactics used by the Russian-backed Internet Research Agency during the 2016 election, when polarizing content regarding American race relations was used to sow discord and animosity.[73] Agents recognized that analysis of historical imagery would be irrelevant in online debates where anyone with a social media account was empowered to draw historical parallels at random drawing on the vast amounts of *e*-history already on the Web. What mattered was how quickly the visual past could be deployed to score political advantage. Foreign disinformation agents used America's past to inflame racial and political divisions. Russian agents flooded social media with content about race in America in 2016, including incendiary Facebook advertisements, Facebook pages, Instagram posts, tweets and YouTube activity on NFL players kneeling for the national anthem and police brutality.[74] Russian operatives excerpted historical imagery from across the Web and repurposed it with inflammatory headlines, running ads on Russian-owned Facebook pages and targeting users with interests in Martin Luther King, African American history, African American Civil Rights Movement (1954, 1968) and Malcolm X. Numerous Russian ads on Instagram linked to the hashtag #africanamericans.[75] Russian accounts on Twitter tweeted with the hashtag #history more than 8000 times in the United States between 2015 and 2018, and more than 1400 times with the hashtag

#blackhistorymonth. Russian trolls even used the hashtag #twitterstorians in some of their tweets.[76] This begs the question of how many tweets by professional historians were in direct or indirect response to foreign influence operations. This would be a fascinating history communication study.

The larger point is to recognize that amid an online environment that had placed the amateur historian on par with the expert, celebrated and lauded the manipulation of nostalgic imagery in our feeds, and granted credibility and authority to virality, the flooding of iconic and arresting imagery that purported to represent history in self-evident forms became a crucial ingredient in information warfare. It became effective because of the attributes of the imagery—not for any analysis, contextualization or critical scrutiny—and because any social media user, activist or foreign agent, could claim credibility by making such nostalgic imagery go viral, crowd-sourcing it into collective consciousness, and asserting that it offered a surface-level understanding that "satisfied" to participate in whatever current debate was ongoing. As my editor said while we worked on this book together, "We think we're learning about history but really what we're seeing is a progression of symbols."[77] A progression of iconic symbols injected into a fast-moving and emotionally charged social Web proved to be potent political weapons.

As e-history became deeper embedded into the fabric of the social Web, it became less and less about the past, and more about how we symbolized to others where we stood in the present. It became a means by which we performed our identities online, reducing content to their obvious plot points and surface-level meanings in order to win heated arguments. They were tools that help set agendas and generate quick reactions. They were useful for their attributes, not their facts.

Such symbolic media products were effective on social media; they were also incredibly poignant in legacy media, which reclaimed power and center stage in the mid-to-late 2010s as *The New York Times*, *The Washington Post*, CNN and other corporate outlets produced news coverage and commentary on the debates raging online and across America. In the case of race in America, such debates were emblematized by the iconographic symbols of Confederate flags and Confederate monuments. Within a competing war of symbols on the social Web, and the privileging of viral and visual symbolic conflicts as a means to attain visibility and influence, the newsworthy past would become another sizable addition to the e-history universe.

CHAPTER 7

The Newsworthy Past

e-history does not solely reside on social networking sites. It extends to media forms that seek to take advantage of social networking in order to gain visibility and influence. *e*-history packages an element, or elements, of the past for consumption on the social Web, and tries to leverage the social Web in order to gain visibility. Throughout the 2000s and 2010s, that included online content related to history produced by news organizations. As the dynamics of the social Web became increasingly intertwined with contemporary news gathering and reporting,[1] the newsworthy past emerged, shaped by the imperatives of Web 2.0: reader-centric, commercially viable, instantly gratifying and extrinsically valuable—worthy for its symbolism and salience as much as (or more than) its accuracy and veracity. Within such an ecosystem, *e*-history related to the current headlines, aligned with contemporary media logic, offered a bite-sized portion of historical scholarship in an accessible form and, ideally, had salience on social media so as to stimulate clicks, views and shares.

The salience of a historically informed news story to the news consumer is critical to whether the newsworthy past sees the light of day. Editors and news producers carry certain assumptions about what their audiences will click on, reinforced by analytics. In large part because of the Web, the reader is presumed to have a short attention span, prefer brevity to length, plain-language to jargon, stories that relate to the latest political headlines, and to have found her way to a piece of content via social media—be it Twitter, Facebook, Google or Reddit. The reader is assumed to prefer the

© The Author(s), under exclusive license to Springer Nature
Switzerland AG 2022
J. Steinhauer, *History, Disrupted*,
https://doi.org/10.1007/978-3-030-85117-0_7

800-word op-ed to 80,000-word book and to not be interested in the scholarly arguments of professional historiography. "It helps to step back and think about it from the perspective of your audience," wrote historian and op-ed contributor Nicole Hemmer in her writing advice to other historians. "It's less about what *you* know and more about what they need to know."[2]

The expertise of historians is central to the construction of this form of *e*-history, but ultimately the end-product must conform to the reader's tastes, not the writer's. Increasingly throughout the 2010s, the news industry viewed itself in competition with the trillions of other pieces of online material. A *New York Times* article lamented in 2016 that an exploding watermelon on Buzzfeed received 10 million views as the reporter wondered aloud how journalists could compete.[3] *e*-history emerged out of this environment, not solely transposing the study of history into the social Web, but into a news ecosystem increasingly being forced to adapt to the Web's sensibilities. Jim VandeHei, a co-founder of *Politico*, told the *New York Times* that the survival of the news industry depended on "giving readers what they really want, how they want it, when they want it,"[4] such engagement critical to selling advertising. "Audience engagement seems to be functioning both as a means and an end," media scholar Philip M. Napoli wrote.[5] The newsworthy past, then, had a built-in imperative to deliver to readers, "what they want, how they want it, when they want it" in a manner that would beget visibility on the social Web.

Being embedded within the news cycle, these forms of *e*-history are also commercial by nature. While the newsworthy past seeks to serve an explanatory function, it must ultimately generate views, likes, clicks and shares. If it does not, it becomes difficult for a media company to justify the time, effort and expense incurred to create it. News corporations, like social media itself, are increasingly data-driven commercial enterprises, with social media and algorithms the dominant factors.[6] News organizations use social data to dictate their reporting, and analytics tell newsrooms which stories are trending online and how long people stay with a story. Algorithms estimate the demand for stories and distribute attention-grabbing articles across social media. Posts that appear to be going viral became more likely to show up in feeds.[7] At one point, *The Guardian* had more than 1000 employees tracking reader page views and time spent on pages.[8] An Australian tabloid experimented with paying journalists a bonus for driving subscriptions and traffic.[9] When *The New Republic* was purchased by a former Facebook executive, he brought with him a data guru whose job was to increase the odds of viral success stories, to watch trending topics on Facebook in order to generate content and to look at data from prior years in order to find traffic-grabbing stories.[10] Gawker Media's Nick Denton wrote in a memo to his staff, "We—the freest journalists on the planet—were slaves to the Facebook algorithm."[11] American journalism is a "cultural enterprise lodged in a commercial enterprise," one media scholar told me[12]; covering what is trending on the social Web helps the commercial enterprise ensure the sustainability of the cultural enterprise. The newsworthy past cannot be divorced from its larger commercial apparatus.

As the newsworthy past responds to current headlines, it is also, by nature, instantly gratifying. The newsworthy past seeks to deliver quick analysis to current headlines in a manner that "satisfices" for the reader, allowing the news organization and the readership to feel as though they have made a contribution to whatever public debates are currently swirling. One Belgian researcher noted that when the COVID-19 pandemic first began in January and February 2020, Belgium's leading newspapers used historical analogies and references in up to 65 percent of their articles to try and contextualize the virus. As the author points out, this conceit was used so often as to be rendered meaningless; the random and varied historical references included everything from SARS and influenza to the Eighty Years War, the 1923 Tokyo earthquake, the development of the Boeing Dreamliner and the Eruption of the Eyjafjallajökull volcano. It became a "randomized grab-bag" of reassuring analogies that offered no instructive analysis to policymakers nor any actionable information to the broader public about the severity of the coming outbreak.[13]

A more meaningful process of gathering, synthesizing and analyzing past evidence for insights might have resulted in more useful findings, but to accommodate the demands of the news cycle, that process must be accelerated. "Over time you get a sense of what's ephemeral and what's going to be in the news cycle for a while," wrote Nicole Hemmer in the same op-ed advice piece. "The ephemeral stuff you have to hop on immediately, and it's very easy to miss the news cycle."[14] The news we see in our social feeds—including *e*-history—is increasingly a highly engineered product: political actors, activists or marketers engineer buzz on social media; news producers watch what online conversations are trending and produce stories on those subjects; historians write op-eds about what those stories mean; then the conversation fizzles out and a new cycle begins. The newsworthy pasts we see are devised by both the historians who pitch their ideas and the editors who consider their pitches in order to fit within these cycles. If such a fit cannot be made, the story will not get published and the historical knowledge contained within it will remain largely invisible to the news-reading public. As a *Washington Post* editor told one historian when rejecting her op-ed pitch, it was "too historical."[15]

The newsworthy past, then, has no intrinsic value to news producers or news consumers. The newsworthy past does not get published solely because it sheds light on the past in a rigorously researched manner. Scholars might agree that a piece of *e*-history meets high standards of veracity, accuracy and integrity. But in the news ecosystem, that does not afford it commercial or editorial value. It has no value unless it can be pegged to a salient news story, is tied to an anniversary, has the potential to go viral, or is visually arresting. An agreement among scholars that a particular article may shine valuable light on the past is irrelevant. The newsworthy past derives its value from the light it shines on the *present*, and how well it can advance the editorial and commercial objectives of the news organization, increasingly determined by analytics. A historian once told me about an article she had published that upset her because it contained a factual error that had slipped through the editing process. The article was deemed a success by the editors because it had more than 64,000 shares.[16] In a Web 2.0 economy predicated on traffic, eyeballs can become more valuable than accuracy.

The newsworthy past also emerges from an evolution in the editorial side of journalism over the past 40 years. As journalism scholar Thomas R. Schmidt writes, "newspapers and news outlets have increasingly moved towards explanatory and contextual reporting over the past three decades and embraced stories that went beyond daily news. Against this backdrop, incorporating historical perspectives has been partly a result of editorial efforts to broaden the spectrum of what counts as news."[17] The embrace of different kinds of stories derives, in part, from the economic pressures of Web 2.0. Newspapers had already been losing readers to television since the mid-1960s, and by the end of the 1980s, there were fewer newspapers and fewer newspaper readers in the United States than there had been in the 1970s.[18] Since the 2000s, online platforms had been gradually extracting significant portions of ad revenues from news publishers,[19] with advertisers migrating as much as 85 percent of their money to Google and Facebook.[20] The lost revenue decimated American newsrooms. From

2001 to 2016, the number of people employed by the newspaper industry dropped nearly 60 percent. Newsroom employees fell 45 percent from 2008 to 2017.[21] At least 1700 newspapers shut down since 2004.[22]

Similar to Jonathan Wegener of Timehop, news organizations realized that history could make for good stories and be good for business. The past offered plentiful content, related to issues readers cared about, broadened the spectrum of what could be considered news, and allowed journalists to claim authority and expertise in an environment where their expertise and authority was being challenged. Media corporations launched an array of history columns and projects during the 2010s. In 2013, *The Wall Street Journal* launched a digital column called "Historically Speaking," authored by biographer Amanda Foreman. Its articles included "Secret Agents, From Babylonian Tablets to Bond" timed with the release of a new James Bond film; "How America's Writers Loved and Hated Thanksgiving," published prior to Thanksgiving; "Comets Chill and Cheer Throughout History," coinciding with a NASA mission to Pluto; and "Resolved to Lose Weight in 2016? Join a Venerable Club," published two days before the New Year. In 2014, TIME.com launched a history section edited by journalist Lily Rothman. The initial purpose was to showcase stories from TIME's corporate archive (a.k.a., a Timehop for the magazine), and grew to include history-themed articles and interviews with historians. The trope of revealing the history you didn't learn in school became a common device for TIME's history section, with headlines such as "You've Probably Heard of the Red Scare, but the Lesser-Known, Anti-gay 'Lavender Scare' Is Rarely Taught in Schools"; "Co-founding the ACLU, Fighting for Labor Rights and Other Helen Keller Accomplishments Students Don't Learn in School"; and "These Latinas Were Pioneers for Workers' Rights in the U.S. Here Are 2 You Should Have Learned About in School." In 2017, *The Washington Post* launched two online history sections: "Retropolis" (run by a journalist) and "Made By History," edited by professional historians. And in 2019, *The New York Times* launched its "1619 Project," which sought to "reframe the country's history, understanding 1619 as our true founding, and placing the consequences of slavery and the contributions of black Americans at the very center of the story we tell ourselves."[23] By the close of the decade, there were tens of thousands of online articles produced under the masthead of news outlets that tied history to current events.

As demand among media producers increased for this type of *e*-history, history communication adapted. Professional historians took their research intended for each other and re-packaged it to link scholarly expertise with trending headlines. This was billed as "history to contextualize current events"[24]; or "current events in historical context"[25]; or "current events in historical perspective"[26]; or "current events into historical perspective"[27]; or "historical background of current events"[28]; and dozens of similar permutations. It became a trend within the history profession in the United States, everywhere from *The Washington Post*'s "Made By History" column to academic projects such as The History News Network, The Ohio State University's "Origins" and the University of Texas at Austin's "Not Even Past." The website Bunk, created by historian and National Humanities medal winner Ed Ayers, was launched in 2017 to amalgamate these various history-as-it-relates-to-current-events verticals into a unified hub.[29] For professional historians, the newsworthy past became a crucial mechanism for achieving visibility and influence on the social Web.

For an example of how this worked in practice, consider the massacre in Charleston, South Carolina, in summer 2015, the tragedy that prompted the Ty Seidule PragerU video. On Wednesday, June 17, 2015, Dylann Roof entered the Emanuel African Methodist Episcopal Church in Charleston, South Carolina, where a group of congregants were holding a weekly prayer meeting. Roof sat quietly with a gun concealed in his possession. An hour into the meeting, he stood up and launched into a diatribe denouncing a black takeover of white America. He proceeded to murder nine people, purposefully leaving one person alive to tell what happened. Then he fled. Roof was identified by security footage and apprehended in North Carolina the following day. By Thursday afternoon, Berkeley County, South Carolina's Twitter account had tweeted an image of Roof wearing a jacket with flags of apartheid-era South Africa and Rhodesia, a former British colony ruled by a white minority.[30] On Saturday morning, two Twitter accounts publicized a website by Roof called "The Last Rhodesian" that included a 2000-word racist manifesto. Photographs on the site showed Roof holding a Confederate flag.[31]

President Barack Obama issued a statement on midday Thursday framing the massacre as part of the broader issue of gun violence.[32] Flags in South Carolina and across the nation were lowered to half-staff. Yet, due to a state law that prohibited the Confederate flag at the South Carolina state capital from being lowered without the vote of the state's general assembly, the Confederate flag in Columbia, S.C., remained at full height. Progressive activists, particularly the NAACP, and Progressive journalists seized on the symbolic juxtaposition of the Confederate flag above the state capital the day after a racial hate crime to reframe media attention and social media conversation toward permanently removing the flag altogether, which the NAACP had advocated for decades. The flag and the legacy of the Confederacy quickly became the compelling news angle for media producers to generate stories, a cycle that would last for months.[33] It was within this media cycle that opportunities for the newsworthy past emerged, connecting historical analysis of the Confederacy to recent events and swirling media debates.

In the wake of Charleston, professional historians whose careers had been dedicated to scholarship on race, the Civil War and the Confederacy found new receptivity for their work. Within a week, scholarship that had likely been unknown to most Americans was suddenly searchable on the websites of *HuffPost*, *The Atlantic*, *The Guardian* and *The Chicago Tribune*, as well as on Twitter, Facebook, Reddit, YouTube and other social media platforms. Historian Manisha Sinha wrote about the history of Charleston's AME church.[34] Historian Douglas Egerton was interviewed about the Charleston roots of nineteenth-century insurrectionist Denmark Vesey.[35] Historian Jason Morgan Ward wrote about the history of "white fear of a black takeover."[36] Because these histories suddenly resonated with a racially charged and symbolically potent political debate, they were more valuable to the news industry than they had been only a week or two prior.

Confederate monuments and iconography continued to be trending news stories for years following Charleston, pushed into the public sphere after the Neo-Nazi rally in Charlottesville in 2017 and the murder of George Floyd by a white police officer in 2020. These dramatic battles in the streets over symbolic markers of race and power offered media producers innumerable history angles to pursue. Historians had written about questions of race in America for decades, but these dramatic and symbolic events, and the corresponding media frenzies, offered highly visible opportunities to showcase that expertise to meet the news cycle's demands. Civil War historian Adam Domby, a professor at the University of North Carolina at Chapel Hill, commented to the *Chronicle of Higher Education* during the school's controversy over a Confederate Silent Sam statue that "business is good."[37] Domby fielded, by his count, 400 emails on the topic of Silent Sam as well as participating in interviews, panels and meetings on the topic.[38] For Ty Seidule, business was also good. Not only did his video on the U.S. Civil War go viral, his book on Confederate monuments titled *Robert E. Lee and Me*, published in the wake of George Floyd's murder, led Seidule to media opportunities, speaking opportunities, book sales and being featured on *CBS This Morning*.[39] Historian Ibram Kendi leveraged his popularization of the term "antiracist" to rise from a visiting professor to an endowed chair in a span of five years, in addition to becoming a CBS News Racial Justice Contributor and Founding Director of the Boston University Center for Antiracist Research.[40]

This is not to impugn Kendi's, Seidule's or Domby's contributions, but rather to point out the pivotal role that the newsworthy past played in their rise to celebrity public intellectuals. During the same period, thousands of other historians produced work on the subjects of anti-Asian xenophobia, Islamophobia, anti-Semitism and other historical discriminations. Yet, the media fixation on the conflict between black America and white America made some histories highly visible in the public eye and rendered others invisible. During the summer of 2020, Kendi and other historians published regularly in *The Atlantic*, *The New York Times*, and CNN on the subject of race in America; meanwhile the Times opinion editors told other historians that op-eds about anti-Semitism were "not a good fit for us at this time."[41] Just as Ken Burns's *Civil War* documentary in 1990 helped Shelby Foote—one of the historians interviewed—sell 100,000 books in six months,[42] so did the newsworthy past on issues of white supremacy, race and Confederate iconography help a select number of American historians sell more books, open new academic centers and advance their careers.

For professional historians, then, demonstrating that historical scholarship had *extrinsic* value to the news media helped to make the broader case for history's *intrinsic* value to society. Did that message get through? A common theme in our journey across the *e*-history universe has been that despite the massive proliferation of *e*-history throughout the 2000s and 2010s, history enrollments continued to decline and funding for professional history continued to be constrained. The proliferation of the newsworthy past has not led to a massive increase in university enrollments or improvements to the professional history job market. One effect has been, rather, the conflation of history with journalism in the eyes of the general public. Members of the American public see historians as "journalists of the past" who report on the past in the same way that journalists report on the present.[43] Some members of the public cannot distinguish a historian from a journalist; an educational consultant I spoke with identified

Princeton historian Kevin Kruse (he of "Twitterstorian" fame) as a journalist and sent me his op-eds on MSNBC.com as proof—in the process also eliding the distinction between a reporter and an op-ed contributor.[44] The blurring of history and journalism has, in fact, drifted Americans' definitions of history further away from how professional historians define their work. As revealed by the 2020 Frameworks study, Americans do not see history as an ever-evolving intellectual argument that analytically and interpretively examines evidence from the past.[45] The newsworthy past has pushed professional history to become a *presentist* discipline, one that must make rapid-fire comments about the present in order to be publicly valued information. News headlines are the primary entry points into historical understanding for most Americans. The past has to be applicable to the news apparatus in order to be relevant—lest it be relegated to the dustbin of the news cycle or the back of the course catalog.

The Frameworks study also revealed that the newsworthy pasts were, increasingly, the primary interactions that Americans had with history. This was affirmed by my own in-person interviews, where students, journalists and Silicon Valley professionals confessed to relying on the social media accounts of major news corporations as their primary source for historical information. For social media users and news consumers, the newsworthy past offers a good-enough understanding of events that happened prior. News consumers were "satisficed" with the 800 words they might skim on CNN or *The New York Times*, rarely (if at all) engaging with the 80,000-word book. The effect has been to elevate certain histories into American popular consciousness that directly inform current political crises—the Civil War, Civil Rights, race relations, American Conservatism—while burying other histories that do not, such as maternal charity in France, the Ottoman Empire in World War I, nineteenth-century Russian writers or Indigenous communities in Bolivia. An argument can be made for why all these topics are intrinsically valuable to study, but unless an argument can be made for why they are *newsworthy*, 99 percent of Americans will never learn about them.

A third effect has been to make it more profitable and possible for journalists to publish commercial books about the past, particularly the Presidency. The term "Presidential Historian," frequently used in contemporary news analysis, is, in fact, a media creation, coined by journalists.[46] An array of journalists, news media personalities and pundits have self-proclaimed themselves to be "Presidential Historians" without possessing history degrees or history training.[47] Authors and journalists such as the late Cokie Roberts and Naomi Wolf have written books or spoke publicly about the past under the pretense of having the authority of a historian, only to misstate facts or misinterpret critical evidence.[48] The credibility of being a journalist has served as a stand-in for making authoritative claims about the past without needing to earn such credentials via history education (after all, anyone can do it!). During the same period that bloggers without journalism degrees and "fake news" websites self-proclaimed themselves to be journalists—so, too, did journalists without history degrees or history training self-declare themselves to be historians. The same journalists decrying fake news and social media for disrupting professional journalism were, simultaneously, part of a trend of journalists disrupting professional history![49]

For news organizations, then, the prestige and credibility of e-history content served, principally, to bolster the news industry itself. The embrace of the newsworthy past was part of how professional journalism responded to the competition for eyeballs, advertising dollars, status and authority posed by the rise of social media. Political scientist Corey Robin deemed this the "Historovox," a conflation of the short-term needs of journalism with the long-term erudition of scholarly expertise.[50] The result, as Robin put it, draws on the authority of academia for the purpose of validating a piece of journalism. (This is one reason why the professional historians one typically sees in national newspapers and newscasts reside at Ivy League universities such as Harvard, Yale, Princeton and Columbia. Those pedigrees are symbolic ways to validate the importance of a news story.) For professional historians—who were often compensated modest amounts or not compensated at all for their contributions to the newsworthy past—the benefits were principally visibility, writing for non-expert audiences and the opportunity to showcase their activism, opinions and subject matter expertise.

Like all e-history operating within an image economy, appearing in the news media became as much a *symbolic* act as an *educational* one for historians. It connoted prestige and credibility, making an implicit argument for the value of professional scholarship. As we've seen throughout this book, the social Web has forced historians to fight to retain their epistemic authority against Wikipedia, @HistoryInPics and History Cool Kids. The newsworthy past allowed professional historians to differentiate themselves from the amateurs not solely by offering historical facts—which could be found in multiple places—but by offering historical *perspective*. Those historical perspectives could not be gleaned from Wikipedia or

@HistoryInPics; the magazine of the American Historical Association is called *Perspectives* for this reason. Being recognized for those perspectives via news outlets such as CNN, *The Washington Post* or *The New York Times* reinforced a hierarchy of who should speak with authority about the past and who should not.

The *New York Times* "1619 Project" offers a fitting conclusion to this analysis. The "1619 Project" was initiated by *New York Times* journalist Nikole Hannah-Jones, who had previously worked for ProPublica and *The Oregonian*.[51] The project brought together a cross-section of journalists, activists, academics and artists to argue that 1619—not 1776—marked the true starting date for the American republic, the date of 1619 chosen to coincide with the 400th anniversary of the first African captives arriving in the British colony of Virginia. The news hook of a 400th anniversary—an extension of the "On This Day" or "This Week in History" content—justified the newsworthiness of the package. Academics and public intellectuals served to validate the premise. Contributors included sociologist Matthew Desmond, writer Clint Smith, columnist Jamelle Bouie, historian Kevin Kruse, attorney and activist Bryan Stevenson and several other poets, journalists and artists—none of whom are historians of early America. The project was not premised, then, on historical expertise around the date of 1619; it was premised on using the past to tap into an ongoing, highly symbolic, politically charged debate; advance the editorial and commercial objectives of the newspaper; and deliver provocation, novelty and surprise.

There were both supporters and critics of the project.[52] But the more relevant point for our purposes is to recognize the "1619 Project" as a media creation: instigated by a journalist; timed to an anniversary; relying on the media logic of being novel, unexpected and controversial; and executed by a network of activists, academics and journalists who were selected not for their expertise on the year 1619 but their social media followings, name recognition, pedigree, and their willingness to accept the predetermined premise of the package. Once the project went viral on social media, the *Times* leaned in to maximize on the revenue: developing curriculum, producing merchandise, printing extra copies of the magazine and devoting more column space to it. The premise was also re-packaged for live events and a book project. The salience of ongoing political crises offered an opportune moment for a commercially produced project invoking the past to become a media sensation. Interestingly, the *Times* never credited Project 1619 Inc. which was founded in 1994 by descendants of those African captives and had spent a quarter of a century attempting to publicize the historical significance of that date to American history. Project 1619 in fact, wrote on its website, "In August the New York Times produced a magazine and podcast on their views on 1619 and its after life. Project 1619 Inc. was not consulted or involved in their production. Project 1619 Inc. does not support or endorse their opinions."[53] Meanwhile, Hannah-Jones, leveraged the commercial success of her project to command professional speaking fees, become a tenured professor, and win a Pulitzer Prize. Journalists, like technologists, have found much opportunity in the past.[54]

The collision of all of these dynamics—the desire of historians to retain authority, the desire of journalists to retain cultural relevance, the battle of news organizations to generate revenue, and the need to produce stories that appeal to short attention spans and fast-moving news cycles—created the conditions for the newsworthy past to emerge. Each piece of content encompassed these dynamics, whether news consumers were aware of them or not. The particular circumstances of the 2010s—the Trump presidency, racial violence, demonstrations by White Nationalists and corresponding counter-protests—strengthened connections among historians, journalists and activists during the period. But as Nahon and Hemsley write in *Going Viral*, clusters that form on social media around common interests can dissipate once that common interest disappears.[55] Will these networks remain durable in the coming decade? That is unknown. For media companies, business models remain the primary challenge. Those models will continue to be under strain as the Web evolves. Historians have helped corporate media organizations such as *The New York Times*, *The Washington Post*, *Politico*, TIME, CNN and *The Wall Street Journal* solidify their dominance of the news industry by contributing their expertise to these platforms, often for little or no compensation. Ultimately, for professional history to continue to be featured in corporate journalism it must be good for business—both the editorial and the corporate sides of the organization.

The Washington Post's "Made By History" column offers a fitting epilogue in this regard. "Made By History" operates as an independent blog published under *The Washington Post* masthead. The *Post* does not pay the professional historians to edit the column and offers only a portion of the column's advertising revenue back to the editors. As a result, the column has not yet been able to pay contributing historians for their articles.

While a few "Made By History" columns receive tens of thousands of page views, those metrics are small compared to other news stories that garner millions of views. Advertising dollars, thus, do not cover "Made By History's" costs, and no donors have come forward (at time of writing) to fully underwrite the project. Though it has fared better than Nupedia or the Ultimate History Blog, "Made By History" has struggled as a viable business model—even as it has succeeded in publishing thousands of op-eds by historians. "Made By History" may, ultimately, shut down if it continues to be economically unsustainable. Business models matter.

If content about the past—by journalists, historians, activists or others—does not generate clicks, advertising dollars, foundation grants or reader interest, it will not gain airtime or column space in corporate media or on the social Web no matter its merits or scholarly rigor. On the social Web, little survives due to its intrinsic value. In a digital marketplace, extrinsic value—measured in engagement metrics—is the determining factor. Apart from financial challenges, there remain content pressures as well. *e*-history in the news media must be a "good-enough" form of history that appeals to commercial tastes, not so rigorous or academic so as to be inaccessible. If it conforms to commercial tastes and media logic, it can gain visibility. If not, it will remain invisible.

Many news organizations today function, for all intents and purposes, as think tanks; *The New York Times*, *The Washington Post*, TIME, *Philadelphia Inquirer* and ESPN feature podcasts, conferences, live-streamed events, YouTube channels, subscriber-only newsletters, in-house commentators, dozens of verticals, options for book and movie deals, and endless streams of content delivered to consumers by algorithms embedded within the social Web.[56] Major news corporations are moving away from exclusively written columns and into multi-media. If news publishers do not think that professional historians can deliver engaging content in these formats and help advance their evolving business objectives, professional history will risk being left behind. If *e*-history content does not generate audience response, it will struggle to receive column space or air time. In particular, the evolution of journalism into podcasting in order to find new audiences and enrich its bottom line led to the medium being valued at more than $9 billion by the end of 2019.[57] As journalists increasingly speak about the past via podcasts, helping to further expand the purview of what gets considered news, it has brought with it another expansion of the *e*-history universe, the storytelling past.

CHAPTER 8

The Storytelling Past

The history podcasts that reach our eyes and ears via the social Web tend to be predicated on the storytelling past, a form of *e*-history that seeks to activate the emotions and curiosity of the listener and that relies on human interest, whimsy, wonder and storytelling, as opposed to rigorous scholarly argument. Like other forms of *e*-history, the storytelling past succeeds by positioning itself as an antidote to professional history, rescuing the past from the clutches of experts. The values of professional history are not what are sold, nor what make the podcast commercially viable. "Instead of names and dates, let's focus on the narrative," podcaster Adam Bleskie says at the beginning of his history podcast, HI101. "The goal is to make connections, to foster curiosity and to appreciate how incredible the story of humanity really is. I'm not an expert, and this isn't a lecture. This is HI101."[1]

Podcasting is as much a product of the social Web as Facebook or Twitter—and the podcasting boom has paved the way for a new form of social media, dubbed "social audio" and manifested on platforms such as Clubhouse, Twitter Spaces, Soapbox and dozens of similar apps. Some of these platforms will fold and others will endure, yet combined with podcasting they add even more *e*-history to an already crowded universe. The "untapped opportunity in the past" that led to the rise of digital nostalgia apps in the early 2010s also led to the creation of hundreds of history podcasts by the end of the 2020s. A search of the Apple podcast store in 2020 returned more than 240 history podcasts—and that did not include

J. Steinhauer, *History, Disrupted*, https://doi.org/10.1007/978-3-030-85117-0_8

limited-run history podcasts from NPR, Slate, *The New York Times* or *The Washington Post*.[2] The sub-Reddit r/HistoryPodcast lists even more history podcasts, including a podcast on the history of Africa; a Muslim perspective history podcast; a podcast on Cambodian history and the Khmer Rouge; a "Human Histories" podcast launched by "two dudes"; a podcast called "One Mic Black History" centered on "little known events or persons from African American history"; "HI101"; a "History of the Cold War" podcast; "Hardcore History" with Dan Carlin; "Revolutions" by Mike Duncan; "The American History" podcast with Shawn Warswick; Dan Snow's "History Hit"; "The History of WWII Podcast" by Ray Harris, Jr.; "The History of the Twentieth Century" by Mark Painter; a "History of The Great War" by Wesley Livesay; a history of the crusades podcast by Sharyn Eastaugh; and the "The Fall of Rome" podcast by Patrick Wyman.

Similar to Wikipedia, @HistoryInPics or History Cool Kids, much of this *e*-history podcasting positions itself as a relief from professional history. HI101 is explicit that its show "isn't a lecture." A student newspaper described the popular "Stuff You Missed in History Class" as information that "does not come across like a normal history class lecture."[3] One podcast was simply titled "History That Doesn't Suck."[4] Being a relief from professional history—or a relief from the perception of professional history—remains a hallmark of *e*-history across platforms and formats.

Surprise also works as a conceit in *e*-history podcasting just as it does in other genres of *e*-history. One podcast listener said that surprise was an element common to the history podcasts he enjoyed. He enjoyed Malcolm Gladwell's "Revisionist History" podcast because he was surprised by what Gladwell found. He enjoyed a BBC history podcast because it had "surprising stuff" that he didn't know. One podcast is titled "History Impossible: Historical Events And People You Wouldn't Believe."[5] The popular "Stuff You Missed in History Class" podcast was originally titled "Fact or Fiction? History Stuff for the History Buff."[6] One Mic Black History claims to cover "little known events or persons from African American history."[7] *The Washington Post*'s "Retropod" podcast billed itself as a show for history lovers, "featuring stories about the past, rediscovered."[8] Indeed, history podcast listeners I spoke to gravitated toward shows that surprised them with subjects they were previously not aware of, or things that they did not remember being covered in school. Similar to the premise of @HistoryInPics or @Retronaut, entire shows are built around the conceit that events from history have been forgotten, omitted or deliberately concealed.

The storytelling past harnesses the mechanics of the social Web in order to attract a broad listenership, and like other *e*-history, relies on particular tactics to keep listeners engaged. The most widely listened-to podcasts purposefully place the listener experience at the forefront. In the parlance of this book, then, popular *e*-history podcasts are user-centric, not expert-centric. Successful *e*-history podcasts are built around what makes the best show, not necessarily the most rigorous scholarly analysis or the foremost scholarly expert. Like all media, history podcasts are carefully wrapped packages that construct a version of the past for a particular purpose, in this case to hook a listener. Success in doing so can be engineered if it adheres to particular formats. One producer I spoke with stated that 44 minutes was a "tried and tested" length for a podcast, with the content broken up into segments. That pacing offered a three-story act with a beginning, middle and end that was "very satisfying for a listener."[9] Podcasts that have a narrative structure and are divided into segments are often more effective than extended interviews (though there are exceptions).

Much successful *e*-history podcasting (though not all) also has a commercial imperative at its roots. Podcasting is big business; the global podcasting market size was valued at $9.28 billion in 2019.[10] By the end of 2019, Spotify users alone had streamed more than 700,000 podcasts,[11] with Spotify reporting that podcasting was central to its business model.[12] Within the news industry, podcasting has become a means for journalists and pundits to find new audiences, increase revenue and expand their personal brands. Freakonomics Radio emerged from the NPR affiliate station WNYC in 2009 and spun off as an independent media company in 2018. The success of Freakonomics inspired other podcasts that use the social sciences and the humanities as "fertile land from which stories can be harvested."[13] The BBC History Extra Podcast was launched in 2007 out of the BBC History Magazine. The podcast is produced by the editorial team and has a close relationship with the magazine's editorial and commercial objectives. "Its massive benefit has always been as a big marketing tool for us," said the podcast's creator.[14]

The storytelling past is not solely confined to podcasting, of course, just as "On This Day" content was not confined solely to Facebook. Using storytelling as a means to gain visibility and attract audiences on the social

Web is linked to changes in journalism, wherein storytelling has become a dominant trend. Journalism in the mid-twentieth century followed a convention of leading with a who, what, when, where and why. But as journalism faced competition from television and, later, the Web, using personal stories and narrative tactics became a preferred method for journalists to hook readers by turning sources into characters, events into plots, learning narrative techniques from writing coaches and re-imagining their work "from stenography to anthropology."[15] That style of reporting has spilled over into journalistic podcasting, as well as other segments of society. "Storytelling" has been a booming industry during the Web 2.0 era, with storytelling events such as The Moth and The Storytellers Project encouraging individuals to tell anecdotes from their personal lives; candidates for office structuring campaigns around storytelling;[16] storytelling billed as a method to improve marketing results;[17] and communications firms helping companies frame their corporate communications around stories. It is from this milieu that the storytelling past emerged, an extension of the storytelling fad that has rippled across all forms of media production, shaping and changing how history is taught, told and absorbed.

The storytelling past creates an instantly gratifying effect for the listener. The best storytelling podcasts reward the presumed short attention span of the Web 2.0 consumer by constantly offering "insights per minute," according to one veteran podcast producer.[18] Another podcast producer I spoke with said that he did not listen to any podcasts beyond 30 minutes in length. His particular pet peeve was when the first ten minutes of a podcast was "B.S.'ing about things I don't care about."[19] Professional podcasts get right to the point, putting the most immediate and ear-catching elements at the top and sprinkling in revelations along the way. Podcasting, like a Google search or the hyperlink, offers the shortest distance between two points.

History podcasting also reveals how extrinsic value plays a central role in the visibility of audio formats on the social Web. A popular form of *e*-history podcasting relies on providing historical context to the news cycle, per the previous chapter. Perhaps the most successful show in this genre was Backstory with the American History Guys. The podcast was funded by the Virginia Foundation for the Humanities and co-hosted by initially three, and later four, university professors. It claimed a radio audience of 40,000–50,000 listeners per week and a regular podcast audience of 150,000 people.[20] From its launch in 2008 until its sunset in 2020, it counted nearly 9 million downloads. The podcast's success led to the hosts earning a recurring segment on NPR's "Here and Now," in which the historians were asked by reporters to be historians-on-demand for the given news topic of the week. Many podcasts by professional historians served as extensions of the newsworthy past, using a connection to current headlines as a way to demonstrate the value of history more broadly. The Urban Historians podcast tied scholarship in urban and metropolitan history to current events. The Who Makes Cents podcast on the history of capitalism began by tying scholarship to present-day events before proceeding to a 45-minute interview with a historian.[21] Most recently, the podcast Now & Then featuring historians Heather Cox Richardson and Joanne Freeman "breaks down the week in news and looks back at historical parallels to help us understand our present."[22] The combination of the newsworthy past and the storytelling past merges the desires of media producers with the sensibilities of the social Web in order to gain visibility in both.

The podcasts created by professional historians have by-and-large featured historians in conversations with other historians, extensions of the conversations that historians have with each other. In other words, these professional history podcasts have been expert-centric. While each show touched on a variety of subjects, at heart they were each concerned with history *promotion*—or, sometimes, *historian promotion*. They adhered to a logic that if more people heard historians talking to one another about their scholarship, more non-historians would see the overall value in the field.

Sample of podcasts by professional historians

Backstory Radio	**Began**: 2008
	Format: Historians in conversation with other historians
Making History podcast	**Began**: 2010
	Format: Historians in conversation with other historians
Ottoman History podcast	**Began**: 2011
	Format: Historians in conversation with other historians
15-Minute History	**Began**: 2012
	Format: Historians in conversation with other historians
Footnoting History	**Began**: 2013
	Format: Historians in conversation with other historians
The Junto Cast	**Began**: 2013
	Format: Historians in conversation with other historians
Urban History podcast	**Began**: 2014
	Format: Historians in conversation with other historians

(*continued*)

(continued)

Who Makes Cents	**Began**: 2014
	Format: Historians in conversation with other historians
Ben Franklin's World	**Began**: 2014
	Format: Historian in conversation with other historians
Past Present	**Began**: 2015
	Format: Historians in conversation with other historians
The History Buffs	**Began**: 2015
	Format: Historians in conversation with other historians
The Way of Improvement Leads Home	**Began**: 2015
	Format: Historians in conversation with other historians
Working History	**Began**: 2015
	Format: Historians in conversation with other historians
In the Past Lane	**Began**: 2016
	Format: Historians in conversation with other historians

These podcasts had varying degrees of success in reaching a wide listenership. Contrast that to many of the podcasts structured around the storytelling past, which attained greater visibility due to their alignment with media logic and the values of the social Web. Broadcast networks, media relationships and marketing budgets matter, too: Spotify has much greater capacity to distribute podcasts than an assistant or associate professor teaching a full course load. But as with @HistoryInPics, @Retronaut and Wikipedia, the storytelling past has seen some of the most successful history communication done by journalists, amateurs and hobbyists who apply the conventions of the social Web to information about the past, without concern for credentials.

The most famous example is, perhaps, Dan Carlin and his podcast, "Hardcore History." Carlin is a former television reporter and producer.[23] Begun in 2006, his "Hardcore History" podcasts delved into empires, wars, death and carnage. In many ways, his podcast preempted the military history accounts on Instagram—focusing on dramatic and violent episodes in the past in a decidedly masculine fashion. For many listeners, that was how they conceptualized history, despite the prominence of social history and gender and women's studies in the field today. History was about wars, struggle, conquest and heroism, often enacted by men in power. As one male fan of the show remarked to me, he enjoyed "Hardcore History" because it focused on moments when the world changed. "That's the way I think," the listener admitted.[24] "Hardcore History" leaned into these tropes as opposed to deconstructing them.

Another journalist-turned-history-podcaster was Malcolm Gladwell. Gladwell's history podcast was called "Revisionist History." Launched in 2016, it purported to explore elements of the past that were forgotten or misremembered. In an interview, Gladwell claimed that his podcast would "move people emotionally."[25] Indeed, in a puff piece in *The Guardian*, one writer applauded Gladwell for the way that his podcast was "shocking, absorbing and angering" and that "Gladwell seems to go through the same emotions while presenting them."[26] Gladwell had a formula, much like @Retronaut: appeal to emotions such as whimsy and wonder; lean into human interest; claim to surface what had been buried or forgotten; and place a heavy emphasis on a journalistic brand of storytelling. Like @Retronaut and @HistoryInPics, Gladwell promised to fill in gaps left open by professional historians, telling you what your teachers didn't tell you, adding excitement to your boring history class or taking advantage of what history professionals had not discovered. There are scores of history podcasts predicated on this premise, promising to reveal things that are lesser known, forgotten, little remembered or less discussed. They promised to be the antidote to your run-of-the-mill history. Successful *e*-history often succeeds precisely because it is "off-brand" from typical history.

Sample of history podcasts, hosted by non-historians

Hardcore History	**Began**: 2006
	About: Created by former journalist Dan Carlin; each episode spends several hours chronicling wars, conflicts, conquest and political leaders (kings, emperors, military generals).
HistoryPod	**Began**: 2006
	About: An "On This Day" podcast written and presented by Scott Allsop, a high school history teacher in Romania.
The Bowery Boys	**Began**: 2007
	About: Created by friends Thomas Meyers (music licensing for Sony) and Gregory Young (online travel business). Conversational podcast that tells stories about people or places in New York City.
Stuff You Missed in History Class	**Began**: 2008
	About: Hosted by Holly Frey (former hair salon manager) and Tracy V. Wilson (editorial director); formerly part of the HowStuffWorks infotainment network (founded by a computer programmer); sold to Discovery; sold to a financial services company; purchased by iHeart Media; storytelling podcast that purports to unearth what may not have been covered by high school history teachers.

(*continued*)

(continued)

The Memory Palace	**Began:** 2008 **About:** Created by Nathan DiMeo (formerly of public radio), narrative podcast that purports to tell lesser-known historical stories.
The History Chicks	**Began:** 2011 **About:** Launched to tell overlooked stories of women from the past. "Any resemblance to a boring history class is purely coincidental!" per its official website. Hosted by Beckett Graham (a visual merchandiser) and Susan Vollenweider (blogger and newspaper columnist).
AskHistorians (via Reddit)	**Began:** 2013 **About:** A podcast created by Arthur and Chris, the moderators of the AskHistorians sub-Reddit, "by history nerds for history nerds." Featured members of Reddit's AskHistorians community as well as professional historians.
American Military History Podcast	**Began:** 2015 **About:** Hosted by a man named Justin, a storytelling podcast about American military battles and American men and women in the U.S. Armed Forces.
American Biography	**Began:** [unknown] **About:** Hosted by Thomas Daly (from New Jersey), a storytelling podcast, part of Agora podcast network, "looks at American history by following the course of human events and examining the lives of important, if less discussed, Americans."
Revisionist History	**Began:** 2016 **About:** Malcolm Gladwell's podcast, produced by Pushkin Industries, which promises to reinterpret stories from the past, "something overlooked. Something misunderstood."

The storytelling past raises familiar questions as other forms of *e*-history. One point of contention underlying all *e*-history has been whether or not the amateur historian should practice history in public without the credentialed expertise to do so. In podcasting, this question can also be inverted: should an expert historian who is an amateur in podcasting launch a show without the requisite audio storytelling expertise? As podcasting has professionalized, the standard of audio quality, narrative storytelling and show artwork has professionalized along with it. These factors help to dictate which history podcasts come to our collective attention. (Apple, for example, will not feature a podcast unless it has professional artwork associated with it.) Must an expert historian also be an expert storyteller and expert audio engineer in order to host a successful podcast? Can skilled storytellers who have audio expertise but no subject matter expertise be trusted history communicators? Is technical expertise more or less coveted and prestigious than subject matter expertise?

Podcasts, too, are very much a social media, creating allegiances of insiders versus outsiders. Podcast communities form like-minded clusters that allow some people in and keep others out; podcast personalities become virtual companions to their listeners, and listeners find community and like-minded people through such programming.[27] Anecdotally, I found this to be true among my friends. One friend admitted that he very much enjoys a podcast of two Gen X-ers analyzing movies, yet he cannot listen to podcasts of millennials discussing the same films. One show creates a community of insiders that he feels he belongs to, the references and language recognizable to him; the other makes him feel like an outsider. This supports scholar Sarah Florini's finding that podcasts are quite resistant to intrusion from those outside of their targeted audiences.[28] Much like Twitter, podcasts forge networks around common interests and like-minded clusters. Research suggests that people use the social Web to find people who are similar to them[29] and that Web users seek to follow people who are on similar journeys.[30] Podcast listeners, then, tend to gravitate toward shows on topics they already have an interest in or relate to a journey they are already on. A friend of mine who is a psychiatrist, a parent and politically engaged listens to podcasts about psychiatry, parenting and politics. Another friend interested in sports and movies listens to podcasts about sports and movies. Another friend who watches a lot of television listens to podcasts about TV shows. This suggests that if listeners are not already predisposed to be interested in history, their likelihood to join a podcast community centered around history will be lower.

To reach beyond such like-minded clusters requires a purposeful and concerted effort—efforts that are not always compensated or rewarded by the Ivory Tower or public history institutions. It also requires assistance from weak ties to reach beyond like-minded users into other segments of society. For these reasons, a broader audience is more difficult to achieve for the professor or museum curator, especially if her professional life is encased within an ecosystem away from a major media center. In general, the average podcast has 130 listeners per month. Slightly more than 5 percent of all podcasts have more than 5000 listens per month. The top 1 percent of all podcasts have more than 30,000 listens per month.[31] Visibility in podcasting is dominated by a small percentage of shows, a few predicated around "the past" but seldom around "history."

The explosion of the podcasting industry at the end of the 2010s paved the way for "social audio," a new format of social media that rapidly emerged in the public eye in 2020 and 2021 via the social media app Clubhouse. Clubhouse is a social network based on voice, a hybrid between an on-demand conference call and an on-demand podcast. Launched in March 2020, by March 2021 it had more than 10 million active users, had raised $100 million in venture capital and was valued at $1 billion. At any given time, more than 1000 conversations were occurring around the world in dozens of languages. Similar apps included Twitter Spaces, Sonar, Chalk, Space, Stereo, Soapbox, Yalla and The Cookout. One technology consultant called social audio a "Goldilocks" medium, more rewarding than text but not as draining as video.[32]

I began a History Club on Clubhouse in August 2020 that functioned as a hybrid between a call-in radio show and a podcast. The show was not based on the storytelling past but rather on examining historical and media literacy subjects each week and discussing them in an open forum with listeners from around the world. To my delight, the format found some receptiveness and visibility; the followership grew to exceed 100,000 users. Yet, as Clubhouse grew in popularity, the app became increasingly dominated by conversations about Internet marketing, cryptocurrencies, stocks, personal branding and celebrities. Steadily, my History Club became less visible in the feed, the algorithm surfacing other types of content to users based on their pre-selected interests. With each new social media platform that adheres to logics of the social Web, the values and assumptions of Silicon Valley become further reified—and professional history becomes further buried in the feed, having to work that much harder to achieve visibility.

The proliferation of history podcasts, like other genres of *e*-history, has further embedded the conventions of *e*-history into public conceptions of the past, leading major media organizations and bloggers to shift the very definition of history to one about storytelling as opposed to scholarly argument.[33] Those who rely on the storytelling past as a stand-in for all historical knowledge prefer the history that is off-brand from the traditional history classroom, offers surprise and novelty, activates emotion and human interest and is listener-centric as opposed to expert-centric. The podcast listener seeks to explore on his or her own, to be led on a journey and to not be told by the expert how or what to think. "I don't accept the historian opinion," one history podcast listener told me. "I form my own opinions."[34] For this reason, the podcast listeners I spoke to often skipped interview podcasts where experts talked with other experts. They opted, instead, for podcasts that had dynamic hosts, displayed rapport and chemistry among guests, and referenced things they could relate to. In other words, they gravitated toward the *attributes* of *e*-history, as opposed to its accuracy. One podcast listener I spoke to expressly stated that he did not enjoy the conversation format between fellow historians. "If I want to shoot the shit about history, I can call a friend," he said.[35] That friend may soon be a robot, our final piece in the expanding *e*-history universe.

CHAPTER 9

History.AI

Joseph Mah is an engineer working to automate everything. According to his LinkedIn page, he created a bot that can make YouTube compilations of 35 different video game streams and upload them automatically. A script finds and rates the clips based on their contents and viewer interactions, edits them together and uploads a final video. It uses machine learning to categorize the clips, scrapes metadata from Twitch to tag the videos and processes them via Amazon Web Services, integrating with search engine optimization tools. The completely automated YouTube channel had 75,000 unique views per day in June 2020.[1]

How AI will affect the histories we see, the histories we learn and professional historians is, perhaps, best approached through this example. To date, the majority of the *e*-history across Web 2.0 has been created by humans leveraging technologies and algorithms. A portion of future *e*-history, perhaps a sizable portion, created on Web 3.0 will be produced by machines. It is not difficult to imagine how engineers such as Mah could automate a process that locates historical content in Wikipedia, the news media, on Twitter or in podcasts; categorizes the content through machine learning; scrapes the metadata; and produces new *e*-history content by the thousands. The most visible and accessible *e*-history of the future may have little-to-no human involvement in its creation.

The AI we interact with today is Artificial Narrow Intelligence (ANI), wherein computers perform specific tasks as well, or better, than humans.

© The Author(s), under exclusive license to Springer Nature
Switzerland AG 2022
J. Steinhauer, *History, Disrupted*,
https://doi.org/10.1007/978-3-030-85117-0_9

Such AI applications include recruiting employees;[2] boosting restaurant sales;[3] analyzing X-rays;[4] drafting emails;[5] or solving a Rubik's cube.[6] In these instances, computers are not pre-programmed with all the possible outcomes, but rather learn over time to produce optimal results via algorithms powered by datasets. In the case of fast-food restaurants, data about what foods people eat at which times of the day—when fed into algorithms—produce highly specific menu recommendations for each individual. This is one example of how a contextual Web is being integrated throughout society. Whereas the first iteration of the Web mirrored an office—with static desktops, folders and files—and the next iteration featured networks, the third iteration of the Web is principally concerned with flows and streams of information.[7] History on the Web—or more precisely, e-history flowing across the Web—will be no exception.

The widespread adaptation of the automated past could mean that information about the past we encounter will be highly contextual, delivered to us by machines at precise moments based on our unique circumstances. For example, a car equipped with a machine learning console could determine based on our GPS coordinates, our listening history and our political leanings that while driving across the American South we want to hear stories about either enslaved Africans or Southern plantation owners. Using a virtual assistant, the car will deliver the content to us before we ask for it. A smart oven in our home will sense an ingredient in the food we're cooking and tell us a historical fact about its uses. Conversational AI will help our children with their history homework by answering questions they have not yet thought to ask. Smart televisions will detect our mood, stress levels and viewing patterns and, without asking, turn on a historical documentary to either ease our minds or stimulate our emotions. Using AI, our devices will learn all the elements of our lives—details, moods, emotions and patterns—and use that data to deliver highly contextual e-history content tailored to each of us. This algorithmically delivered e-history will only be as accurate, evidence-based and interpretive as the content it can find in its datasets. The sources will include the massive amounts of e-history already strewn across the Web. As that e-history already dominates search results, AI will privilege that content and distribute it even wider, further and deeper throughout society.

This is already happening. Google's in-home assistant currently scrapes the Web like a browser, using sorting algorithms to surface answers to what you've queried for. Amazon's Alexa operates similarly: it turns a voice question into text, uses machine learning to do intent extraction and then scrapes huge datasets that Amazon has purchased in order to find an answer. Some answers come from proprietary datasets whose contents are entirely opaque to the broader public. Some answers come from Alexa Answers, an Amazon-created, crowd-funded platform where anyone can submit their own answers to questions, gaining reputation scores along the way. Some answers come from Wikipedia. A friend admitted that when he searches for historical information using Alexa, he knows the top answer often comes from Wikipedia yet he does not stop to think to question its accuracy.[8] The more seamless these technologies become in delivering information, the more likely we are to accept it without scrutiny.

Search engines can also generate automated answers to queries in paragraph form, as opposed to generating a list of websites. The semantic search engine SenseBot can mine billions of websites to produce a short summary of an answer to a question. When I typed "Who Discovered America" into the SenseBot search box, the AI returned a 20-sentence summary of Christopher Columbus with footnotes linking to the websites from which it retrieved the information: WorldAtlas.com (founded by a map enthusiast and today run by a Web entrepreneur); ZMEScience.com (founded by a science journalist from Romania); AllThatsInteresting.com (whose founder also started the comedy site Runt Of the Web); HistoryPlex.com (owned by content aggregator Buzzle); Listverse.com (a website of listicles); and an NPR segment from 2007.[9] One could imagine a high school or college student using such an AI on a homework assignment; the e-history sources listed above—none of them from professional historians—would form the basis for the essay. AI uses the data it has available to deliver an answer in the most user-centric and instantly gratifying way possible regardless of whether the material comes from a journalist, hobbyist, Wikipedia contributor or actor with a political or economic agenda. If AI cannot find an answer from the Web or in its datasets, it will not be included—meaning volumes of literature by professional historians in printed books or behind academic paywalls might never be considered.

The challenges posed by AI go beyond disseminating incomplete historical understanding, or historical understanding at odds with professional scholarship. It also includes the production of historical content. An omnipresent fear in popular reporting about AI is that it will displace existing occupations, making entire industries obsolete. This could include professional historians. Such AI is called Artificial General Intelligence (AGI), and while some engineers have suggested it remains a distant concern,[10] others predict it is only 5–20 years away.[11]

Elements of AI already exist that could replace or displace professional history. A principal role of the historian is to conduct research. However, AI has proven it can discern patterns in massive quantities of data that human beings cannot. AI could analyze billions of historical documents in ways that no human ever would have the stamina to do. Machines could review terabytes of sources and decipher patterns in the past that no historian could ever uncover. It could review millions of documents from a Presidential administration to find insights into political decisions. It could review billions of Wikipedia entries for biases or trends. It could synthesize the 82 percent of journal articles in the social sciences that are never cited, and recognize patterns in the scholarship that were previously ignored.[12] An AI historian could do *better* research than a human historian ever could.

A second principal role of the professional historian is to write. AI can do that as well. In August 2019, *Foreign Affairs* reported on an artificial intelligence program that generated a news story on a foreign policy issue that was indistinguishable from one written by a human.[13] The tool, GPT-2, used probability to predict which words should logically follow the next in a given sentence. Over long stretches of text, after analyzing millions of Web pages, the program used predictive technology to write an entire story. As explained by researcher Simon Smith, GPT-2 could take millions of biomedical papers and write a new paper in the style of a published researcher that would potentially be indistinguishable from other scientists.[14] It could do the same for a history article. With the next iteration of the tool, GPT-3, one blogger produced an article that was upvoted to the top of a popular website—meaning that an article written by AI was elevated in people's feeds by AI and used by AI to answer human questions.[15] AI could not only analyze millions of research articles, it could also distill them into an article more efficiently than a single historian ever could—an article that could rise to the top of the Google search rankings and be considered a reputable source by other AI. AI could also learn how to think like a historian, developing a strategy similar to how it learns to be a better poker player.[16] It could produce scholarly articles in a matter of days or weeks, far faster than professional historians who spend years on a single submission.

A third principal role of the professional historian is to teach. AI could assemble a history textbook based on the information it finds in datasets and on the Web via Wikipedia, Reddit, Quora and Google, among others, as well as in publications such as *The New York Times, The Washington Post,* NPR or *The Atlantic*. It could analyze millions of Wikipedia pages and formulate a curriculum that highlights the most important events in a particular decade based on a given set of criteria (e.g., length of an entry, number of entry contributors, number of footnotes, number of page views, number of citations and user engagement). History lessons could be curated entirely through machine learning and narrated by voice assistants. One AI researcher estimated there will be 1 billion users of personal friend robots with teaching abilities in the next decade—robots that are not task-based but rather sense the moods and aptitudes of children and learn to develop individualized teaching strategies.[17] AI could write the next History AP exam and score it. Some universities already use AI to collect information about their students, analyzing their learning patterns to improve outcomes. AI could use that data to develop lectures that keep students from getting bored; structure course loads for students based on analyses of past course loads; or design syllabi based on data from student performance and student attention spans. AI could grade papers, give tours of plantation or historic houses and analyze the architectural data about a historic site. History lessons could be personalized to each participant; history classrooms may no longer need to exist. There may be no need for universities to have history professors on payroll. Investments in AI could make the majority of tenured history faculty expendable. Only a handful of adjunct professors would be needed to perform tasks that AI could not. Brick and mortar institutions would become irrelevant as AI-driven online education proliferates.[18] The credentials that historians have spent decades achieving would be less relevant as more tasks are outsourced to machines.[19] Anything about the past we wish to analyze, synthesize or teach might be possible via AGI. AGI could lead to the history-education business being outsourced almost entirely to technology companies, with only a need for a handful of consultants on hand to review the work. Historians could be among this century's displaced workers, perhaps even a displaced industry.

These technologies will also shape the types of history content that gets created. The platforms and devices will reward and incentivize new forms of e-history that can be delivered in new formats and in even shorter, fragmentary and individualized manners. Humans and AI will respond by developing genres of history communication that optimize for these technologies in order for their data to rise to the top of the feed. The technological choices being made today are already changing how we will learn history moving forward. "The things we call technologies are ways of building order in our world," wrote Langdon Winner in 1980.[20] They establish frameworks that can last for generations.

A secondary technology that may shape the future of history is the blockchain. The applications of blockchain technology are still early, and though uncertain, its future applications have potential to be wide-ranging. The values that underpin the blockchain matter as much as its protocols. Reminiscent of Wikipedia, the blockchain is meant to be entirely decentralized; there is no core authority that dictates truth to other participants. The blockchain is not stored in any single location; participants in a network take shared ownership of that network and all participants are envisioned to have a stake in being accountable for actions on the chain, regardless of their credentials. When one user wants to initiate a transaction with another, millions of other computers distributed around the world work to verify it. The verified block is added to the chain, which is then stored across millions of computers. A unique record of the transaction is created that becomes indelible because changing one unique transaction in the chain requires changing the entire chain—which, because it is not stored in any centralized location, is exceedingly difficult. As such, the blockchain promises a future of the Web that is decentralized, transparent and immutable.[21]

The applications of blockchain technology are most apparent to financial transactions. Allowing unique and indelible peer-to-peer transactions offers security and eliminates a broker taking a percentage. Exchanging stocks on the blockchain removes trading commissions. Purchasing products on the blockchain removes credit card fees and bank fees. One blockchain investor described to me the potential security applications in nations with unstable legal systems. In her case, her family in Pakistan could transfer land deeds on the blockchain, creating an indelible record that could not be manipulated by a corrupt government.[22] But blockchain developers are also beginning to examine applications in other areas. In 2018, Forbes experimented by integrating blockchain technology into its journalism. The project was undertaken with a company called Civil, which aspired to use blockchain to improve the financial stability, reliability and permanence of journalism. Though Civil was absorbed into another company in 2020, other journalism projects are leveraging the blockchain, as well as projects in science, medicine, law and publishing.

How this will affect the study of history is too early to tell. However, there are some hints. Blockchain could become a method for museums, archives and libraries to preserve metadata about their collections. A decentralized catalog record on the blockchain could replace a database system, for example. It could save museums money and resources by no longer having to build, purchase or maintain proprietary software on their local servers. All catalog information could be recorded on the blockchain and searchable to many more people, not to mention granting community members stake in the museum, allowing broader access to museum collections, making provenance and custody timelines transparent, and lowering museum overhead. Blockchain could also affect academic publishing and university presses. Currently, university presses pay miniscule amounts of royalties to scholars, if they pay royalties at all. In the future, scholars could bypass academic publishers and publish their work directly on the blockchain. The blockchain could generate a unique record of publication, and the book or article could be sold directly to consumers. Academic writers would receive direct compensation for their work, eliminating university presses altogether.

The blockchain has potential to also write history. An Ethereum project called Historians DAO has already empowered a cohort of community members to research and authenticate Non-Fungible Token (NFT) transactions that may be "historic" to artists and buyers. These are not professional historians whose singular authoritative voice based on years of credentials empowers them to draw conclusions about past events. Similar to Wikipedia or the *netto uyoku*, these are a cross-section of devoted and active users who deliberate in public on a Discord server and crowd-source their way to consensus through upvoting. The agreed-upon consensus can then be published by anyone on the blockchain, becoming a canonical record. The more decisions that become canon, the more a historian improves his or her reputation score and can monetize his or her expertise.[23] Blockchain users can carry reputation scores that are crowd-sourced and crowd-generated, similar to Lyft drivers or Airbnb hosts. Holding and maintaining a position of authority within a blockchain community correlates with your score. As in other parts of the Web, authority is tied to *how* one contributes, not solely *what* one contributes. Ironically, the notion of unique record permanently stored on the blockchain with no possibility for revision contradicts the discipline of professional history. Revision is endemic to the practice of history; professional history is constantly evolving, and as new sources emerge, the narratives about the past get revised. Ironically, then, the blockchain's promises of permanence are innately ahistorical. But much like on Wikipedia, Twitter, Instagram, the news media and podcasting, the creation of blockchain *e*-history already does not require the involvement of professional historians, nor does it adhere to the same set of professional values. As Web 2.0 evolves into Web 3.0, and expands into every aspect of our lives, the path that Wikipedia started us on two decades ago might displace professional history altogether.

CHAPTER 10

Does History Have a Future?

A journey across the World Wide Web reveals the breadth of the *e*-history universe as well as why some history content has reached our eyes and others have not. With each new platform and media trend that emerged, capturing money and public attention, new forms of *e*-history emerged with them. Wikipedia pages, #OnThisDay factoids, @HistoryInPics tweets, Twitter threads by historians, Instagram posts from History Cool Kids and war-themed accounts, newsworthy op-eds, podcasts, Clubhouse rooms, TikTok videos, YouTube channels, and content about the past created by machines all compete for our online attention under the name of "history." Some *e*-history is created by professional historians; others by journalists, hobbyists, teachers, teenagers, political operatives, hostile foreign actors, blockchain users and computational programs. Some *e*-history has educational intent; some has nefarious intent. All are driven by agendas, be it the promotion of a person, a brand, an ideology, a discipline or a set of values. Different *e*-history rely on different mechanisms to achieve visibility and influence: crowd-sourcing, digital nostalgia, virality, visually arresting, newsworthy, storytelling or via AI. But the most visible and influential *e*-history tend to mirror the values of the Web itself. The chief result has been not a more sophisticated understanding of the past among non-historians that rely on the social Web for information, but rather the embedding of the values of the social Web deeper into our lives, the characteristics of *e*-history coming to represent *all* history, online and offline. *e*-history has made the practice of history chiefly about the changing

J. Steinhauer, *History, Disrupted*, https://doi.org/10.1007/978-3-030-85117-0_10

conditions for visible Web content rather than discerning with fidelity and rigor what may have happened in the past.

The resulting e-history landscape compels individuals across the globe to make sense of this dizzying universe of material created by a myriad of actors with an array of agendas, in no chronological order, atomized as part of millions of feeds, rising and falling in visibility and urgency with the news cycle and popularity of different platforms, and with little-to-no assistance on how to evaluate and interpret it. Take, as one example, the Australian teenager Essena O'Neill. In 2015, news articles circulated online about how O'Neill accumulated 800,000 followers on Instagram and then promptly quit the platform. Before doing so, she criticized the curated nature of social media by sharing the "real stories" behind the images she'd posted during her three-year "Insta-career."[1] She renamed the account "Social Media Is Not Real Life" and added she was "both addicted to social approval and terrified no one would value me for myself."[2] Her trajectory had a post-script, though, that did not receive as much media attention. She re-emerged on the Web in 2019 with a new project called "Authority Within." The site was a dizzying maze of e-history videos on subjects such as neo-liberalism, wage slavery, capitalism, consumerism, Karl Marx, Noam Chomsky, Imperial America and Celebrity Worship. The mish-mash of content included YouTube videos from The School of Life (launched in 2010 by a consortium of psychotherapists and now with 600+ million channel views); The Big Think (launched in 2006 by two former producers of The Charlie Rose Show and now with 300+ million channel views); Cuck Philosophy (launched in 2017 by Jonas Ceika and with 8+ million channel views); the anarchist Leftist channel Angie Speaks; the leftist channel Mad Blender; Halim Alrah (whose tagline is "radicalize yourself and those around you"); and Russia Today, the Kremlin's propaganda channel.[3]

O'Neill confessed she had been "struggling" since stepping away from Instagram, "working many shitty jobs" and missing the celebrity and adoration she once had.[4] She responded by consuming pseudo-academic and conspiratorial explainer videos from the far left and the far right. The content she consumed, which radicalized her in a kind of patchwork fashion, was largely e-history content that offered surface-level understandings and confusing rambles that posed as sophisticated analysis. e-history cobbled together from across the Web without structure, curation or media literacy can lead any of us to darker places, especially among the vulnerable and impressionable.

As *e*-history has proliferated, professional history has struggled. Between 2008 and 2018, history majors declined by 33 percent, a steeper drop than any other discipline measured (though it has rebounded slightly). History majors declined in all segments of society for all races and genders at all types of institutions.[5] History PhDs declined as well.[6] In an era dominated by the social Web, and facing reduced enrollments and reduced funding, the argument that professional history rests on its own merits—that is, it has intrinsic value—has fallen flat. The Web is outcomes-based. That something can be a good in-of-itself without producing a useful end-product has become an increasingly difficult argument to make, including to college students deciding a major. And the vast amount of *e*-history instantly available fuels a growing perception that history can be self-taught. One person I interviewed admitted sheepishly that she now thought *all* history could be self-taught.[7] Participants in a Clubhouse conversation agreed that as history can be learned on your phone, history education should *solely* be a self-education.[8] The study of the past has been completely disrupted by the Web, forced to demonstrate its extrinsic value to other segments of society lest it be relegated to the dustbin of the news cycle or the back of the course catalog.

Will professional historians become relics of a bygone era? Prior to the nineteenth century there were no professional historians as we think of them today. The coalescing of a professional guild in the nineteenth and twentieth centuries led historians to be minted in high numbers through a linear path of credentialism: high school degree, college degree, graduate degree, apprenticeship and, finally, acceptance into the profession. Just as the Web has upended linear reading so, too, has it upended linear credentialism. In the twenty-first century, requiring specific credentials to speak publicly about the past feels increasingly incompatible with the direction of the Web. A communications environment wherein journalists, celebrities, activists, public officials, TV hosts, filmmakers, Wikipedia editors, blockchain enthusiasts, tech entrepreneurs, teenagers and foreign misinformation agents all represent as historians online existentially challenges how long the linear credentialism of yesteryear can maintain its gatekeeping power. It's possible that the role of the professional historian will change substantially or disappear entirely. That prospect adds an ominous threat to a field where currently the average salaries are low; the business models are under strain; and unstable, part-time and temporary work are ubiquitous.[9]

These existential threats are not confined to professional history, of course. Technology and the Web have disrupted other areas of expertise, as well. A 2019 article in *The Atlantic* by contributing editor Jerry Useem chronicled a change aboard the USS Gabrielle Giffords: no expert sailors on the ship. A large number of sailors each with expertise had evolved into fewer "hybrid sailors" who were jacks-of-many-trades. Useem noted that this model appeared in other segments of society where employers encouraged employees *not* to become experts, but rather to be nimble, flexible and quick-thinking generalists. Expertise was an obstacle, not an asset. That made Useem uneasy, he wrote. "The more we invest in building and embellishing a system of knowledge," Useem said, "the more averse we become to unbuilding it."[10] Professional historians have invested tremendous energy, time and effort into building and embellishing a system of knowledge that codifies their approach to analyzing and interpreting the past. The social Web, Wikipedia, Instagram "flop accounts" and shifts in how citizens—particularly younger citizens—decide where and how to confer authority have been unmooring forces, the consequences still unfolding.

Throughout the rise of *e*-history, humanities scholars have argued for the intrinsic value of their work, and that devaluing their contributions is injurious to democracy and calamitous to society. Humanistic expertise is the "real" type of expertise that one college president lamented the Web had made "irrelevant," a "potentially dangerous" turn of events, in his estimation.[11] Humanistic authority is critical to ensuring a properly functioning world—or at least, a world wherein the knowledge and power of the subject matter expert is privileged. But it is not so much a death of historical expertise the Web has engendered, but a belief that the distinction between the expert and amateur historian is now immaterial. After the murder of George Floyd in 2020, Alex Cequea (an animator and former marketing executive) and Tara Jaye Frank (a consultant who formerly worked at Wal-Mart) used available *e*-history to create their own *e*-history content related to race in America, circulating viral videos and booking lucrative speaking gigs.[12] Neither they nor the individuals and corporations that consumed their content demanded to see their academic credentials.

The professional historian now must differentiate herself not by what she knows but rather by how she *interprets* what is known. It is not historical knowledge, but rather *historical thinking* that differentiates the historian from the average citizen, the perspectives that historians offer in op-eds and on podcasts what differentiates them from the amateur or the hobbyist. Such skills must be honed and sharpened, it is argued, via credentials and training, hence how the history profession draws boundaries around itself, boundaries that are "patrolled and protected at all costs against outsiders," to quote one senior historian.[13] On the Web, professional historians have tried to patrol and protect these boundaries against @HistoryInPics, Dinesh D'Souza, Dan Carlin and others. But with so much *e*-history available, and more destined to be created, building a wall around the discipline may be a losing battle. Some historians continue to insist that only "scholars and smart people" should speak publicly about the past. The social Web says otherwise.

To retain or regain their authority on the decentralized Web will require history scholars and practitioners to operate as parts of broader conversations. The chorus of voices matters, which is how Twitter became an effective platform for professional historians during the Trump administration. The more historians on a platform amplifying a message, the more it appears that a crowd-sourced consensus is being formed. That dynamic repeated across Facebook, Instagram, YouTube, Twitch, TikTok, Clubhouse and future social media networks could make professional history increasingly visible on a decentralized social Web. Historical scholarship is already an iterative process; historians in academic and public history edit, peer review, collaborate and gain feedback from colleagues constantly. Yet, the final product gets published under a single author's name. That should change as single-authorship is no longer an imprimatur of authority among a growing portion of the broader public. Anyone who contributed to the creation of a piece of scholarship should not only publicly be acknowledged, but the record of collaboration should be published and time-stamped akin to a Wikipedia article or a blockchain transaction. Transparency and community should become the foundational tenets of professional history, each aspect of the scholarly production and dissemination cycle recorded and delineated in a participatory and crowd-sourced manner.

On a decentralized Web, professional historians must also exercise convening authority, not solely subject matter authority. Communicating history extends beyond being a featured expert who writes an op-ed or delivers a public lecture. Communicative power is afforded to those who can convene and organize online communities, empowering members to be front-and-center in their own education and discovery. In such a milieu, communicating one's credentials must take on new symbolic forms. The process of developing and honing historical expertise must become a symbolic act of self-communication if the social Web is to continue to play an outsized role in the histories we pay attention to. The manner by which historians contribute to the conversation will be as important as the substance of what is contributed. Reputation scores or other visible markers of participation will become pathways to social power.

Bringing students back into history courses and history departments is an important aspect of the equation, as is improving the experience of history education. Much column space has been devoted to this topic over the years, an analysis of which would be a separate book. One radical suggestion would be to remove history from the post-high school curriculum and insert it as a requirement after several years in the workforce. As college inexorably shifts to an outcomes-based, job-placement pipeline, some friends I spoke with suggested that they were not ready to study history as an undergraduate operating within such an anxiety-laden environment of high expenses and competitive career competition. Perhaps it makes sense to confer degrees upon students in shorter periods of time at a lower cost, with the caveat that they must return to their alma maters five or ten years later (most likely online) to pay the remaining balance and complete a mini-curriculum in history, historical thinking and history communication. Such a course load, after several years in the professional world, might resonate more with a young or mid-career professional as she sees first-hand the role of history in participatory citizenship. After being exposed to so much *e*-history "in the wild," she may be more mentally, intellectually and financially ready to push beyond it under the guidance of a scholar.

Whenever it occurs, history education must become user-centric. The expectations of modern-day learners have been reconfigured by technology in ways that do not appear to be immediately reversible. History education must place the *user* at the center, not the expert. This applies to social media, in-class instruction, museums and historic sites. That will require creativity to reconceptualize history classes and historic sites in ways that surrender epistemic authority and create crowd-sourced, highly visual, user-centric experiences supplemented by voice- and video-enabled technologies and leveraging AI and the blockchain. I've maintained for several years that these innovations can best be advanced through the field of History Communication, which is why I have founded the History Communication Institute. The History Communication Institute will seek to provide funding to support cutting-edge history communication projects. It will help foster community and online networks that welcome professionals and amateurs alike, building bridges between the journalist, podcaster, museum curator, YouTuber and PhD academic in ways that existing disciplinary boundaries do not allow. It will create opportunities for historians, tech and media to establish mutually beneficial partnerships that serve the interests of policymakers, journalism and the broader public. And it will help Web users become better consumers of historical information online by revealing what agendas are work, what tactics are being used to achieve visibility, and how the platforms help dictate which pasts we encounter and which we never see.

The burden is not solely on professional historians and Web users, though. Web developers, Web designers, Silicon Valley and corporations have a responsibility to ensure that the next iteration of the Web values and prioritizes incentives beyond speed, scale and commerce. The decentralized and semantic Web must incentivize rigor, patience and thoughtfulness, not solely income and enthusiasm. This will be even more crucial as blockchain and AI advance us toward a hyper-individualized Web. Every aspect of our lives is becoming digitized and commercialized: our likeness, our personalities, our relationships, our identities, our tastes, our memories, our assets, our travel and our biology. Companies such as Rally.io even use our social capital as the basis for our own currencies. To corporate America and Silicon Valley, we are each a unique portfolio of data that can be mined for revenue—or that we, ourselves, are compelled to generate revenue from as we are pushed further into gig-work and the creator economy.[14]

In such a milieu, the imperative becomes how to monetize every interaction or calculatingly develop our brand to further increase our market value. Within this environment, e-history will play as meaningful a role on the Web as its ability to be commodified. Historians and history communicators will be compelled to turn their scholarship, content, personalities and likeness into commodities in order to earn a living, a process already underway as fewer and fewer well-paid, full-time jobs are available to those with history degrees.[15] Where interpretive arguments about the past made by professional historians based on time-consuming and rigorous research, which is believed to have an intrinsic value regardless of its potential for monetization, fits into such an online future is unclear—if it fits at all.

The current trajectory portends that the petabytes of e-history thrown onto the Web over the past 25 years will become the foundations for highly individualized and commercialized versions of history education developed and patented by technology companies such as Google, Microsoft and Amazon, curated by AI and drawing upon the vast corpus of crowd-sourced, nostalgic, visual, viral and newsworthy pasts that can be most efficiently retrieved from the Web. That fragmentary and hyper-individualized form of history education in the United States may lead to a greater apathy toward laborious, pain-staking humanities research that has no explicit utilitarian, brand-building or argument-winning function, as well as further declines in history enrollments, history funding and history degrees as history education becomes increasingly outsourced and corporatized. If we continue to privilege the *e*-history that delivers instantaneous results and the shortest distance between two points, our desire to flex the opposite muscles atrophy. If we continue to privilege the *e*-history that helps us win arguments about the present, as opposed to histories that make arguments that help us better understand the past, our desire to support the histories that cannot be immediately mobilized in support of a political, personal or commercial agenda becomes weaker. We over-value the histories that result from speed, enthusiasm, efficiency and media logic and under-value the longer-term work that makes such *e*-history possible. Surface-level understandings of the past become *de rigueur* as a means to build a brand, gain social currency or advance a political agenda. Those selected and edited histories become so privileged in our minds that we lose the ability to think outside of them. Our understanding of the past vis-à-vis history becomes like the stars amid the broader galaxy. A @HistoryInPics photograph or an #OTD factoid is the bright shiny object that we see; but what led up to the photograph and what happened after the event are the dark energy and dark matter that make up 95 percent of the rest of the story. *e*-history shows us the 5 percent of shiny objects and deceives us into thinking we know the whole universe. In reality, it is the space between the shiny objects where the deepest mysteries are, along with the truest understandings.[16]

    e-history has had benefits. It has diversified the various pasts that people are aware of, democratized access to numerous archives, allowed a greater number of actors on social media to create historical content, advanced the careers of several professional historians and generated engagement with the past by people around the world. Yet, while each of the non-historians I spoke with for this book professed to enjoy *e*-history, they confessed that they did not learn much from it. Formulating conclusions about the present based on a do-it-yourself, from-your-phone, surface-level understanding of the past offers no assurances of a meaningful result. In the case of the Belgian newspapers, the muddled grab-bag of historical analogies actually had the deleterious effect of reassuring the news-reading public in Belgium about the COVID-19 pandemic based on a belief that the past and the present would have similar outcomes.[17] Such is the conundrum posed by *e*-history: some is created with nefarious intentions, others with educational intentions, but taken in aggregate it seems to produce no net increase in a more historically informed and media literate citizenry even when it promises the inverse. When millions of people engage in an unregulated activity in a decentralized manner with no agreed-upon standards, best practices or ethics, the result can be the complete opposite of what was intended.

The best history helps us see our blind spots. It reveals to us that we are asking the wrong questions or solving for the wrong answers. It can show us how wrong we were at the time something happened, and how wrong our perceptions were about things that previously happened. That allows us (hopefully) to admit our faults and resolve to do better next time. The *e*-history that only reflects back to us what we already suspect to be right, or is produced to in order to reinforce current headlines or satisfy what's trending on social media falls woefully short in these respects. Humility should be history's most important lesson—which seems incredibly necessary in an era of mass self-communication predicated on commercializing and glamorizing the self. A frenzy to create a Wikipedia page or a slew of history op-eds that respond to an item in the news is not a barometer of importance, lasting relevance or deeper understanding. They are products of a particular media environment that rewards certain actors with visibility and influence if they adhere to a set of logics about the social Web. Those logics will eventually change, and moments that feel significant today due to the engagement metrics of social media will gradually recede from relevance and memory. *e*-history is, in itself, a historical artifact, a product of a particular time, place and circumstances.

So long as our digital economy offers financial reward, societal recognition, political capital and career advantage through the engineering of information on the social Web, it will continue to happen. As social media evolves, those conditions migrate onto new platforms. On TikTok, the hugely popular creator @onlyjayus created a video called "History Facts School Refuses to Teach You." It got more than 1.3 million views.[18] On Clubhouse, three technologists hosted an event titled "US History that sounds fake but isn't!"[19] The conventions of breaking free from the boredom of history class and being surprised by what occurred in the past seem likely to persist on new apps and platforms. But new technologies will not immediately displace older ones, as Andrew Chadwick reminds; multiple forms of history communication will co-exist alongside each other for years and possibly decades to come. Scholarly books and journal articles will not disappear anytime soon. Yet, communications environment whose values in fundamental and purposeful ways are contrary to the discipline have created profound challenges. There have been fundamental shifts, and as Jill Lepore states, "such shifts are, by their very nature, gradual."[20] Such is the case with e-history. While the changes to technology, society and the discipline have been incremental, if we take a step back after two decades of the twenty-first century, the terrain looks very different. The social Web has rendered some of the foundational values of professional history exceedingly difficult to transpose in new settings. To paraphrase Langdon Winner, the social Web is a "political artifact." Its design choices will have lasting effects.[21]

Despite all its challenges and drawbacks, the social Web and social media do present opportunities for professional historians to introduce their expertise into public conversations. Yet, today, many of the legacy institutions where historians reside—universities, museums, libraries, think tanks and governments—are perceived to be incapable of dealing with the profound changes our world is experiencing. These institutions seem weighed down by bureaucracy and paralyzed by their legacies. That has led to further alienation, particularly among younger citizens that express disillusionment with traditional brick and mortar institutions and the careers they enable. It should be no surprise that young Americans (and others around the world) see their best career option to turn inward toward self-reliance. While older generations preach a return to twentieth-century institutional ideals such as civic engagement, national service or tenured professorships, approximately 30 percent of young Americans believe their best path to success is to make viral videos on YouTube.[22] Becoming an Internet celebrity offers protection from the legacy institutions that will force them into "shitty jobs." Essena O'Neill walked away from that, then realized she desperately needed it back.

Within that milieu, the boundaries of what gets to be called history will continue to shift. How we come to know things about the past and from what sources we discover information continue to evolve. This ranges from obvious changes such as searching for information in a physical encyclopedia or local library to now looking it up on our phones; to more subtle and imperceptible shifts in drawing us toward different episodes of the past and away from others due to algorithms embedded within the architecture of social media platforms. The technology and infrastructure of the Web have altered how knowledge about the past becomes introduced into the mainstream. It is not solely the domain of the textbook, the professor or the museum curator. It is the collected will of the crowd. It is the teenager who knows how to engineer social media success with a simple formula. It is the activist who can manipulate the networks in order to make a certain polarizing message about the past go viral. It is the millionaire who can finance a series of Web videos with funding from other millionaires. It is a collection of a thousand images and ideas on a social networking platform associated with a common hashtag. We have all collectively agreed to these shifting means of sense-making and historical knowledge-acquisition through our embrace of these technologies, integrating them willfully into our lives.

Staring into cyberspace, we can now see the contours of the vast *e*-history universe we have all had a hand in creating. In the decades ahead, we will face choices as to what we do with it, in what directions it further evolves, what types of histories and history communicators we support and elevate, and what investments and interventions we collectively need to make in order to foster and promote thoughtfulness, understanding, contemplation, rigor, depth, community, wisdom, grace and inclusiveness. The Web is destined to continue to change the past. Will we be able to change with it?

Notes

Chapter 1

1. Ty Seidule, "Was the Civil War About Slavery?" published by PragerU on August 9, 2015, video, https://www.prageru.com/video/was-the-civil-war-about-slavery/, accessed January 10, 2021; Ty Seidule, "Was the Civil War About Slavery?" published by Prager U on August 10, 2015, YouTube video, https://www.youtube.com/watch?v=pcy7qV-BGF4, accessed January 10, 2021; "Was the Civil War About Slavery?" video posted by Dennis Prager on Facebook, https://www.facebook.com/search/videos/?q=ty%20seidule; search conducted on January 10, 2021.
2. Ty Seidule, *Robert E. Lee and Me: A Southerner's Reckoning with the Myth of the Lost Cause* (New York: St. Martin's Press, 2021), 1.
3. Evan Halper, "How a Los Angeles-based conservative became one of the internet's biggest sensations," *Los Angeles Times*, August 23, 2019, https://www.latimes.com/politics/story/2019-08-22/dennis-prager-university-conservative-internet-sensation.
4. Ty Seidule, "Was the Civil War About Slavery?" published by Prager U on August 10, 2015, YouTube video, https://www.youtube.com/watch?v=pcy7qV-BGF4.

© The Author(s), under exclusive license to Springer Nature
Switzerland AG 2022
J. Steinhauer, *History, Disrupted*,
https://doi.org/10.1007/978-3-030-85117-0

5. See HuffPo writer Rebecca Klein on Twitter, https://twitter.com/ rklein90/status/1318290368329371648; Progressive activist Stacey Burns on Twitter, https://twitter.com/WentRogue/status/1318329309040357377; and Princeton historian Kevin Kruse in Halper, "How a Los Angeles-based conservative became one of the internet's biggest sensations," L.A. Times.

6. "Hunting for subversives in the academy has been a favorite sport of conservatives for at least a century," according to John F. Zipp and Rudy Fenwick. See John F. Zipp and Rudy Fenwick, "Is the Academy a Liberal Hegemony? The Political Orientations and Educational Values of Professors," *The Public Opinion Quarterly*, Vol. 70, No. 3 (Autumn, 2006), 304–326.

7. Theresa L. Miller, Emilie L'Hôte, and Andrew Volmert, *Communicating about History: Challenges, Opportunities, and Emerging Recommendations* (Washington, D.C.: FrameWorks Institute, 2020).

8. Conversation between the author and a college student at the University of Michigan, September 23, 2020.

9. Comment made by a graduate student in Germany during a Zoom conversation on May 22, 2020.

10. Conversation between the author and an international journalist, December 22, 2020.

11. Conversation between the author and a high school student in California, September 16, 2020.

12. Conversation between the author and a college student at the University of Michigan, September 23, 2020.

13. Conversation between the author and a Silicon Valley entrepreneur, October 21, 2020.

14. Conversation between the author and a tech policy analyst, October 17, 2020.

15. Conversation between the author and an international journalist, December 22, 2020.

16. In a survey conducted by the Knight Foundation and the Gallup Organization, it was found that despite the greater availability of information in the digital age, a majority felt overwhelmed rather than better informed. See Sam Gill, "The Price of Progress: How 'Digital Pollution' Is Poisoning Democracy and What We Can Do About It," Knight Foundation, January 22, 2019, https://knightfoundation.org/articles/the-price-of-progress-how-digital-pollution-is-poisoning-democracy-and-what-we-can-do-about-it.

17. Halper, "Los Angeles-based conservative."

18. See Benjamin M. Schmidt, "The History BA Since the Great Recession: The 2018 AHA Majors Report," American Historical Association, November 26, 2018, https://www.historians.org/publications-and-directories/perspectives-on-history/december-2018/the-history-ba-since-the-great-recession-the-2018-aha-majors-report.

19. Schmidt, "The History BA Since the Great Recession."

20. Leonard Cassuto, "Worried About the Future of the Monograph? So Are Publishers," *The Chronicle of Higher Education: Community*, April 2, 2019, https://community.chronicle.com/news/2180-worried-about-the-future-of-the-monograph-so-are-publishers.

21. Conversation with the author, October 17, 2020.

22. Conversation with the author, October 30, 2020.

23. Conversation with the author, January 15, 2021.

24. *The Humanities in American Life: Insights from a 2019 Survey of the Public's Attitudes & Engagement* (Cambridge, MA: American Academy of Arts and Sciences, 2020).

25. Karine Nahon and Jeff Hemsley, *Going Viral* (Cambridge: Polity Press, 2013), 57.

Chapter 2

1. Norman F. Cantor and Richard I. Schneider, *How to Study History* (New York: Thomas Y. Crowell Company, 1967), 243.

2. Comment made by historian Judith Giesberg at the Lepage Center for History in the Public Interest, during an event titled "Revising the Civil War," YouTube video, posted by Villanova University, November 13, 2019, https://www.youtube.com/watch?v=j2NMtn6OvpI.

3. David Hackett Fischer, *Historians' Fallacies: Toward a Logic of Historical Thought* (New York: Harper Torchbooks, 1970), xx.

4. Not all professional historians earn a PhD; some work in museums and archives with a master's degree as the highest education level. This is a source of debate within the history profession; whether a practicing historian requires a terminal degree. I have a master's degree; I do not have a PhD. Because of this, some professional historians do not consider me a "real" historian.

5. Cantor and Schneider, *How to Study History*, 11.
6. G.R. Elton, *The Practice of History* (New York: Thomas Y. Crowell Company, 1967), 49.
7. Walter Isaacson, *The Innovators: How a Group of Hackers, Geniuses, and Geeks Created the Digital Revolution* (New York: Simon & Schuster, 2014), 442.
8. Paul Davison, conversation on Clubhouse, November 24, 2020.
9. Conversation on Clubhouse, November 16, 2020.
10. Conversation between the author and a Silicon Valley entrepreneur, January 8, 2021.
11. Tim Hwang, *Subprime Attention Crisis: Advertising and the Time Bomb at the Heart of the Internet* (New York: FSG Originals x Logic, 2020), preview excerpt accessed via https://us.macmillan.com/books/9780374538651.
12. Isaacson, *The Innovators*, 438.
13. Jacob Metcalf, Emanuel Moss, and danah boyd, "Owning Ethics: Corporate Logics, Silicon Valley, and the Institutionalization of Ethics," *Social Research: An International Quarterly*, Volume 86, Number 2 (Summer 2019), 449–476.
14. Douglas Guilbeault, "Digital Marketing in the Disinformation Age," *Journal of International Affairs*, Vol. 71, No. 1.5, Special Issue: Contentious Narratives: Digital Technology and the Attack On Liberal Democratic Norms (2018), 33–42.
15. See "10 Surprising Civil War Facts," HISTORY.com, updated February 8, 2019, original May 10, 2011, https://www.history.com/news/10-surprising-civil-war-facts; "125 Mind-Blowing Historic Facts & Trivia That Are Almost Too Weird to Be True," Parade.com, October 10, 2020, https://parade.com/1099930/marynliles/history-facts/; and "17 Truly Odd Historical Facts That I Had a Hard Time Believing Were Real," Buzzfeed.com, April 23, 2020, https://www.buzzfeed.com/valezabakolli/wild-historical-facts-that-are-actually-true. All accessed January 4, 2021.
16. Howard Gardner and Katie Davis, *The App Generation: How Today's Youth Navigate Identity, Intimacy, and Imagination in a Digital World* (New Haven: Yale University Press, 2014), 18–19.
17. Facts used to be central building blocks of professional history, but today not all professional historians believe in the centrality of facts. Some are more likely to see facts as a series of stories and interpretations, molded by competitions for political and social

power. To quote one historian: "I think most history faculty I know would shy away from saying anything was a 'fact.'" To quote another: "I don't personally believe in facts. It's all stories and interpretation of what has been recorded which is not the same as what happened. This might be one of the reasons that historians aren't read by the public."

18. John H. Arnold, *History A Very Short Introduction* (Oxford: Oxford University Press, 2000), 13.

19. Douglas Seefeldt and William G. Thomas, "What is digital history?" *Perspectives on History: The News Magazine of the American Historical Association*, May 1, 2009, https://www.historians.org/publications-and-directories/perspectives-on-history/may-2009/what-is-digital-history.

20. Hank Green in a conversation on Clubhouse, August 31, 2020.

21. Facebook comment by a friend of the author, posted on Facebook, February 4, 2016.

22. Katrina Eames (@katrinaeames), Twitter, February 23, 2020, https://twitter.com/katrinaeames/status/12309486110406 98371.

23. Crash Course was initially funded through a grant from YouTube; it was subsequently sponsored by PBS, which helped attract additional sponsorships. See Nina Zipkin, "The Simple Question the Producers of the Wildly Popular 'Crash Course' Ask Themselves When Creating Content," entrepreneur.com, November 7, 2018, https://www.entrepreneur.com/article/322929. Khan Academy received a $5 million donation from Elon Musk, amid other fundraising. See Khan Academy, "Elon Musk $5 million donation to Khan Academy thank you," YouTube video, published January 11, 2021, https://www.youtube.com/watch?v=id_MB2RClG4.

24. Valerie Strauss, "Khan Academy using contractors to check Web site's videos," *The Washington Post*, October 22, 2013, https://www.washingtonpost.com/news/answer-sheet/wp/2013/10/22/khan-academy-using-contractors-to-check-websites-videos.

25. Benjamin M. Schmidt, "The History BA since the Great Recession: The 2018 AHA Majors Report," American Historical Association, November 26, 2018, https://www.historians.org/publications-and-directories/perspectives-on-history/december-2018/the-history-ba-since-the-great-recession-the-2018-aha-majors-report.

26. Theresa L. Miller, Emilie L'Hôte and Andrew Volmert, *Communicating about History: Challenges, Opportunities, and Emerging Recommendations* (Washington, D.C.: FrameWorks Institute, 2020).

27. Interviews conducted by the author between August 2020 and January 2021.

28. Tren Griffin, "12 Things about Product-Market Fit," Andreesen Horowitz, accessed January 2, 2021, https://a16z.com/2017/02/18/12-things-about-product-market-fit/

CHAPTER 3

1. Tim Berners-Lee, "Frequently Asked Questions by the Press—Tim BL," https://www.w3.org/People/Berners-Lee/FAQ.html.

2. Walter Isaacson, *The Innovators: How a Group of Hackers, Geniuses and Geeks Created the Digital Revolution* (New York: Simon and Schuster, 2014), 422.

3. "About American Memory," Library of Congress website, https://memory.loc.gov/ammem/about/index.html. The American Memory project was eventually sunsetted and integrated into the broader Library of Congress online catalog.

4. timothy, "The Early History of Nupedia and Wikipedia: A Memoir," *Slashdot*, April 18, 2005, https://features.slashdot.org/story/05/04/18/164213/the-early-history-of-nupedia-and-wikipedia-a-memoir.

5. timothy, "Early History."

6. timothy, "Early History." https://features.slashdot.org/story/05/04/18/164213/the-early-history-of-nupedia-and-wikipedia-a-memoir.

7. Isaacson, *The Innovators*, 439.

8. Interview with Ward Cunningham, posted as a video on the "Wiki" entry in Wikipedia, https://en.wikipedia.org/wiki/Wiki, accessed January 30, 2021.

9. timothy, "Early History."

10. timothy, "Early History."

11. Wikipedia home page, July 27, 2001, captured by the Wayback Machine, accessed January 29, 2021.

12. timothy, "Early History."
13. Dorothy Neufeld, "The 50 Most Visited Websites in the World," *Visual Capitalist*, January 27, 2021, https://www.visualcapitalist. com/the-50-most-visited-websites-in-the-world/.
14. Sanger attributed this to the burst of the dot-com bubble in 2001 and 2002. See timothy, "The Early History of Nupedia and Wikipedia: A Memoir," *Slashdot*, April 18, 2005, https://features. slashdot.org/story/05/04/18/164213/the-early-history-of-nupedia-and-wikipedia-a-memoir.
15. Daniel Pink, "The Book Stops Here," *Wired*, March 1, 2005, https://www.wired.com/2005/03/wiki/.
16. Comment by bcrowell (177657) on Monday, April 18, 2005 @02:00PM (#12272417) on timothy, "The Early History of Nupedia and Wikipedia: A Memoir," *Slashdot*, April 18, 2005, https://features.slashdot.org/story/05/04/18/164213/ the-early-history-of-nupedia-and-wikipedia-a-memoir.
17. Isaacson, *The Innovators*, 434.
18. Roy Rosenzweig, "Can History Be Open Source? Wikipedia and the Future of the Past," *The Journal of American History*, June 2006, accessed via Academia.edu, July 10, 2021, https:// www.academia.edu/3166721/Can_history_be_open_source_ Wikipedia_and_the_future_of_the_past.
19. Comment by ahoehn(301327)*<.nh.eoh..ta..werdna.>on Monday, April 18, 2005 @01:16PM (#12271843) on timothy, "The Early History of Nupedia and Wikipedia: A Memoir," *Slashdot*, April 18, 2005, https://features.slashdot.org/story/05/04/18/164213/ the-early-history-of-nupedia-and-wikipedia-a-memoir.
20. Comment by AKAImBatman (238306) * <akaimbatman.gmail@ com> on Monday, April 18, 2005 @12:29PM (#12271257) on timothy, "The Early History of Nupedia and Wikipedia: A Memoir," *Slashdot*, April 18, 2005, https://features.slashdot.org/ story/05/04/18/164213/the-early-history-of-nupedia-and-wikipedia-a-memoir.
21. Toby Butler, "History 2.0" in *The Impact of History? Histories at the Beginning of the Twenty-first Century*, ed. Pedro Ramos Pinto and Bertrand Taithe (Abingdon, Oxon: Routledge, 2015), 36.
22. See *Historically Speaking*, Vol. IX, no. 4. (March/April 2008).
23. Andreas Kolbe, "Wikipedia: re-writing history," originally published at http://wikipediocracy.com/2014/10/12/wikipedia-re-

writing-history, accessed via Academia.edu, https://www. academia.edu/8962708/Wikipedia_re_writing_history.

24. "Wikipedia: Size of Wikipedia," Wikipedia, https://en.wikipedia. org/wiki/Wikipedia:Size_of_Wikipedia, accessed March 7, 2021.

25. "Wikipedia: Size of Wikipedia."

26. "Wikimedia Enterprise," Wikipedia, https://meta.wikimedia. org/wiki/Wikimedia_Enterprise, accessed July 10, 2021.

27. Andreas Kolbe, "Wikipedia is swimming in money—why is it begging people to donate?" *Daily Dot*, Published May 24, 2021; Updated Jun 1, 2021, https://www.dailydot.com/debug/wikipedia-endownemnt-fundraising.

28. Timothy Messer-Kruse, "The 'Undue Weight' of Truth on Wikipedia," *The Chronicle of Higher Education*, February 12, 2012.

29. Messer-Kruse, "Undue Weight."

30. Messer-Kruse, "Undue Weight."

31. "January 2016 United States Blizzard," Wikipedia, https://en.wikipedia.org/wiki/January_2016_United_States_blizzard.

32. See the Wikipedia user page for "CycloneBiskit," https://en.wikipedia.org/wiki/User:Cyclonebiskit and the Twitter profile for Brenden Moses, https://twitter.com/cyclonebiskit.

33. See Wikipedia user TheAustinMan, https://en.wikipedia.org/wiki/User:TheAustinMan; Wikipedia user Master_of_Time, https://en.wikipedia.org/wiki/User:Master_of_Time; Wikipedia user LightandDark2000, https://en.wikipedia.org/wiki/User:LightandDark2000; Wikipedia user Knowledgekid87, https://en.wikipedia.org/wiki/User:Knowledgekid87; Wikipedia user Jdcomix, https://en.wikipedia.org/wiki/User:Jdcomix; Wikipedia user Aude, https://en.wikipedia.org/wiki/User:Aude; Wikipedia user Feanorstar7, https://en.wikipedia.org/wiki/User:FeanorStar7; Wikipedia user Jolly Janner, https://en.wikipedia.org/wiki/User:Jolly_Janner, Wikipedia user APK, https://en.wikipedia.org/wiki/User:APK; Wikipedia user Daniel Mietchen, https://en.wikipedia.org/wiki/User:Daniel_Mietchen; and Wikipedia user RJaguar3, https://en.wikipedia.org/wiki/User:RJaguar3. All accessed August 1, 2020.

34. See Nathan Jurgenson, *The Social Photo: On Photography and Social Media* (New York: Verso, 2019) on the self-consciousness of creating the past in the present.

35. Article and edit history for "January 2016 United States blizzard," Wikipedia, https://en.wikipedia.org/wiki/January_2016_United_States_blizzard, accessed July 10, 2021.
36. Rosenzweig, "Can History Be Open Source?"
37. Joseph Langdon, "The Renegade History Of 4chan, From Hentai To The Alt-Right," Ranker.com, May 16, 2018, https://www.ranker.com/list/history-of-4chan/joesph-langdon.
38. Tomomi Yamaguchi, "Xenophobia in Action: Ultranationalism, Hate Speech, and the Internet in Japan," *Radical History Review*, Issue 117 (Fall 2013), https://doi.org/10.1215/01636545-221061.
39. Yamaguchi, "Xenophobia in Action."
40. Daiki Shibuichi, "Zaitokukai and the Problem with Hate Groups in Japan," Asian Survey, Vol. 55, No. 4 (July/August 2015), 715–738, https://doi.org/10.1525/AS.2015.55.4.715.
41. Yamaguchi, "Xenophobia in Action."
42. Howard Leitch, *Wikipedia U: Knowledge, Authority, and Liberal Education in the Digital Age*, (Baltimore: Johns Hopkins University Press, 2014).
43. Andrew Chadwick, The Hybrid Media System, 23.
44. Taylor Lorenz, "Teens Debate Big Issues on Instagram Flop Accounts," *The Atlantic*, July 26, 2018, https://www.theatlantic.com/technology/archive/2018/07/the-instagram-forums-where-teens-go-to-debate-big-issues/566153/.
45. Lorenz, "Flop Accounts."
46. Messer-Kruse, "Undue Weight".
47. Tom Nichols, "How America Lost Faith in Expertise," *Foreign Affairs*, March/April 2017.
48. Andrew Odlyzko, "The Glorious Promise of a Post-Truth World," *Ubiquity*, March 2017, https://doi.org/10.1145/3061712.
49. Ami Sedghi, "Facebook: 10 years of social networking, in numbers," *The Guardian*, February 4, 2014, https://www.theguardian.com/news/datablog/2014/feb/04/facebook-in-numbers-statistics.

CHAPTER 4

1. Svetlana Boym, "Nostalgia and its Discontents," *Hedgehog Review*, 9: 2 (2007).
2. Jonathan Wegener, "The Friendslist Story [Chapter 1]," published on Medium, August 12, 2011, https://blog.jwegener.com/friendslist-is-dead-but-we-re-very-much-alive-c63e9d9dee3c.
3. Jonathan Wegener, "The Friendslist Story [Chapter 6]," published on Medium, October 9, 2012, https://blog.jwegener.com/the-friendslist-story-chapter-6-9115ea8dcc62.
4. See image posted on Laughing Squid, https://laughingsquid.com/wp-content/uploads/4squareand7yearsago-20110329-151036.jpg, accessed January 12, 2021.
5. Mari Sheibley, Flickr, February 19, 2011, https://www.flickr.com/photos/mariss007/5462382659/in/set-72157625971749879.
6. Alexia Tsotsis, "4square&7yearsago Knows Where You Checked-in Last Year," *TechCrunch*, February 21, 2011, https://techcrunch.com/2011/02/21/4squareand7yearsago/?guccounter=1.
7. Sarah Kessler, "What Were You Doing on Facebook, Twitter, Foursquare and Instagram One Year Ago?" *Mashable*, December 19, 2011, https://mashable.com/2011/12/19/timehop/.
8. Alexia Tsotsis, "Timehop, a Time Machine for Your Social Media Updates, Gets $1.1M from Foursquare Founders and Others," *TechCrunch*, January 24, 2012, https://techcrunch.com/2012/01/24/timehop-a-time-machine-for-your-social-media-updates-gets-1-1-from-foursquare-founders-and-others/.
9. Ingrid Lunden, "Timehop founder Jon Wegener replaced as CEO by design lead Matt Raoul," *TechCrunch*, January 14, 2017, https://techcrunch.com/2017/01/14/timehop-founder-jon-wegener-replaced-as-ceo-by-design-lead-matt-raoul/.
10. Josh Constine, "Facebook's Timehop clone On This Day gets 60 million daily visitors," *TechCrunch*, March 24, 2016, https://techcrunch.com/2016/03/24/facebook-on-this-day/.
11. Jonathan Wegener, "The Next Chapter: All Eyes on the Future (err, the past)," Published on Medium, January 24, 2012, https://blog.jwegener.com/the-next-chapter-all-eyes-on-the-future-err-the-past-38474ce7b2b1.

12. Alexia Tsotsis, "4SquareAnd7YearsAgo Becomes Timehop, Takes You A Year Back In Time Through Online Content," *TechCrunch*, January 6, 2012, https://techcrunch.com/2012/01/06/timehop-takes-you-a-year-back-in-time-through-online-content/.

13. Tim Berners-Lee, "HyperText Design Issues: Navigational techniques," November 3, 1992, https://www.w3.org/History/19921103-hypertext/hypertext/WWW/DesignIssues/Navigation.html#6.

14. Theresa M. Senft and Nancy K. Baym, "Introduction: What Does the Selfie Say? Investigating a Global Phenomenon," *International Journal of Communication* 9 (2015).

15. Senft and Baym, "What Does the Selfie Say?"

16. Manuel Castells, *Communication Power* (Oxford: Oxford University Press, 2013).

17. Josh Constine, "Facebook Launches Feeds For Photos, Music, Friends-Only, And More," *Techcrunch*, March 7, 2013, https://techcrunch.com/2013/03/07/facebook-launches-multiple-topic-based-feeds-bigger-images-and-a-consistent-design-across-devices.

18. Josh Constine, "Facebook Will Launch Content-Specific News Feeds, Bigger Photos and Ads on Thursday," *Techcrunch*, March 5, 2013, https://techcrunch.com/2013/03/05/facebook-news-feeds-launch/.

19. Josh Constine, "Hands-On with the New Facebook and its Boredom-Killing Feeds [TCTV]," *Techcrunch*, March 7, 2013, https://techcrunch.com/2013/03/07/hands-on-with-the-new-facebook-and-its-boredom-killing-feeds-tctv.

20. On the Facebook algorithm, see Josh Constine, "Facebook Explains the Four Ways it Sorts the News Feed and Insists Average Page Reach Didn't Decrease," *Techcrunch*, November 16, 2012, https://techcrunch.com/2012/11/16/facebook-page-reach/.

21. Stated by Jonathan Wegener during a conversation on Clubhouse, December 3, 2020.

22. Wegener, "All Eyes on the Future (err, the past)."

23. Tsotsis, "4SquareAnd7YearsAgo Becomes Timehop,"

24. Colleen Taylor, "Memolane, the Internet Time Machine, Announces Abrupt Shutdown as Team Joins Unnamed Company," *Techcrunch*, February 21, 2013, https://techcrunch.

com/2013/02/21/memolane-the-internet-time-machine-app-for-exploring-past-social-network-content-is-shutting-down/.

25. This Day in History, Reddit, https://www.reddit.com/r/ThisDayInHistory/, accessed January 13, 2021.

26. Max Farley, Krista Pollett and Brian Whetstone, "Managing social media, doing public history," *History@Work*, December 5, 2019, https://ncph.org/history-at-work/social-media-and-public-history/.

27. UR Daily History website, https://urdailyhistory.com/about-urdailyhistory, accessed March 16, 2020.

28. Today in History (@URDailyHistory), Twitter, https://twitter.com/URDailyHistory, accessed November 24, 2021.

29. Historrically YouTube channel, https://www.youtube.com/user/tyatesor/videos, accessed February 8, 2021.

30. Tsotsis, "4SquareAnd7YearsAgo Becomes Timehop."

31. Facebook had been experimenting with a memories feature since late 2010, but their "On This Day" app was an obvious copy of Timehop. The Timehop app launched within Facebook in 2011. Facebook launched its own version in 2015. See Josh Constine, "Facebook Memories Shows Users a Year by Year Summary of their Activity," *Adweek*, December 16, 2010, https://www.adweek.com/performance-marketing/memories-year-summary-activity/.

32. Josh Constine, Facebook's Timehop Clone "On This Day" Shows You Your Posts from Years Ago, *Techcrunch*, March 24, 2015, https://techcrunch.com/2015/03/24/facehop/?_ga=2.6773 3522.268947925.1610488116-1856212248.1608682002.

33. See Nathan Jurgenson, *The Social Photo* (New York: Verso, 2019) and Svetlana Boym, "Nostalgia and its Discontents," *Hedgehog Review*, 9: 2 (2007).

34. This caption appeared underneath a Facebook post by a friend in March 2020 as she re-posted a photo of her son from two years earlier.

35. Boym, "Nostalgia and its discontents."

36. Boym, "Nostalgia and its discontents."

37. Yasmin Ibrahim, "Instagramming life: banal imaging and the poetics of the everyday," *Journal of Media Practice*, 16: 1 (2015), 42–54, https://doi.org/10.1080/14682753.2015.1015800.

38. Max Boot, "Here's how to Counter the Populist Politics of Nostalgia," *The Washington Post*, last modified May 28, 2019, https://www.washingtonpost.com/opinions/2019/05/28/heres-how-counter-populist-politics-nostalgia/.

39. Douglas Guilbeault, "Digital Marketing in the Disinformation," *Journal of International Affairs*, Vol. 71, No. 1.5, Special Issue: Contentious Narratives: Digital Technology And The Attack On Liberal Democratic Norms (2018), 33–42.

40. Audentes Fortuna Iuvat, "Duterte 2016: Roadmap to Victory," *Pompee La Viña*, June 12, 2015.

41. Davey Alba, "How Duterte Used Facebook To Fuel the Philippine Drug War," *Buzzfeed News*, September 4, 2018.

42. Maria A. Ressa, "Propaganda War: Weaponizing the Internet," *Rappler*, October 3, 2016, https://www.rappler.com/nation/propaganda-war-weaponizing-internet.

43. Boym, "Nostalgia and its discontents."

44. See Ernest Sternberg, *The Economy of Icons: How Business Manufactures Meaning* (Westport, CT: Praeger Publishers, 1999).

45. Timehop website, https://www.timehop.com/about, accessed January 13, 2021.

46. Andrew Liszewski, "'Deep Nostalgia' Can Turn Old Photos of Your Relatives into Moving Videos," *Gizmodo*, February 26, 2021, https://gizmodo.com/deep-nostalgia-can-turn-old-photos-of-your-relatives-1846363190.

47. MyHeritage, "Abraham Lincoln Discovers His Family History on MyHeritage," video published on YouTube on February 11, 2021, YouTube, https://www.youtube.com/watch?v=kEtiajHLmQY.

48. Mansoor Iqbal, "Twitter Revenue and Usage Statistics (2020)," Business of Apps, updated: December 5, 2020, https://www.businessofapps.com/data/twitter-statistics.

Chapter 5

1. Matt Novak, Aussie Teen Behind Viral Sensation @HistoryInPics, Gizmodo AU, January 24, 2014, https://www.gizmodo.com.au/2014/01/viral-sensation-historyinpics-is-run-by-two-teens/.

2. Alexis Madrigal, "The 2 Teenagers Who Run the Wildly Popular Twitter Feed @HistoryInPics," *The Atlantic*, January 23, 2014.

3. HistoryInPics (@HistoryInPics), Twitter, https://twitter.com/Historyinpics, accessed October 24, 2020.
4. Sinan Aral and Dylan Walker, "Creating Social Contagion Through Viral Product Design: A Randomized Trial of Peer Influence in Networks," *Management Science*, Vol. 57, No. 9, (September 2011), 1623–1639.
5. Nicholas Carlson, "How Twitter.com Went from A $7,500 Domain to A $3.7 Billion Company," *Business Insider*, December 15, 2010.
6. American Library Association, "The Business of Social Media: How to Plunder the Treasure Trove," *Reference & User Services Quarterly*, Vol. 51, No. 2 (Winter 2011), 127–132.
7. Karine Nahon and Jeff Hemsley, *Going Viral* (Cambridge: Polity Press, 2013), 16.
8. Nahon and Hemsley, *Going Viral*, 21.
9. Nahon and Hemsley, *Going Viral*, 23.
10. Nahon and Hemsley, *Going Viral*, 31.
11. Xavier Di Petta, "How to learn history in 140 characters," TEDxTeen, YouTube video, published June 3, 2015, https://www.youtube.com/watch?v=aa8FtXCs48E.
12. Nahon and Hemsley, *Going Viral*, 86–89.
13. Retronaut website, https://retronaut.com/about/, accessed January 4, 2019.
14. Matt Novak, "Frequently Wrong @HistoryInPics Company Gets $2 million from investors," *Gizmodo*, December 22, 2014.
15. "All Day Media," *Crunchbase*, https://www.crunchbase.com/organization/all-day-media.
16. Xavier Di Petta, "How to learn history in 140 characters," TEDxTeen, YouTube video, https://www.youtube.com/watch?v=aa8FtXCs48E. Statistics as of October 24, 2020.
17. For an argument against @HistoryInPics by a professional historian, see Rebecca Onion, "Snapshots of History: Wildly popular accounts like @HistoryInPics are bad for history, bad for Twitter, and bad for you," *Slate*, February 5, 2014, https://slate.com/human-interest/2014/02/historyinpics-historicalpics-history-pics-why-the-wildly-popular-twitter-accounts-are-bad-for-history.html.
18. Mashable was sold in 2017 to Ziff Davis, a digital media subsidiary of the tech company J2. Retronaut was subsequently removed

from the site. In 2019, Retronaut was sponsored by Considerable, a "financial and lifestyle brand." Considerable was created by journalist Diane Howard, the former editor-in-chief of *Money* magazine. See Peter Kafka, "Ziff Davis has bought Mashable at a fire sale price and plans to lay off 50 people," *Recode*, December 5, 2017, https://www.recode.net/2017/12/5/16735262/ziff-davis-mashable-sold-50-layoffs-pete-cashmore as well as the homepage of Considerable, https://considerable.com, accessed January 4, 2019.

19. Nicholas Carlson, "How Twitter.com Went from A $7,500 Domain to a $3.7 Billion Company," *Business Insider*, December 15, 2010.

20. See Rebecca Onion, "Snapshots of History: Wildly popular accounts like @HistoryInPics are bad for history, bad for Twitter, and bad for you," *Slate*, February 5, 2014, and Sarah Werner, "it's history, not a viral feed," *Wynken de Worde*, January 26, 2014, http://sarahwerner.net/blog/2014/01/its-history-not-a-viral-feed.

21. Rebecca Onion, "Snapshots of History."

22. See Jonathan Jones "'Retronauting': why we can't stop sharing old photographs," *The Guardian*, April 14, 2014; and Emma Jacobs, "Haunted by the past, in digital form," *Financial Times*, January 23, 2015.

23. "Mix it Up: Cultural Literacy Resources" newsletter, published by School Library Journal, May 2016.

24. Eugene McCarraher, *The Enchantments of Mammon: How Capitalism Became the Religion of Modernity* (Cambridge, MA: The Belknap Press of Harvard University, 2019), 3.

25. New York Almanack web page, https://newyorkhistoryblog.org/about-page/.

26. The Ultimate History Project "About Us" page, https://ultimatehistoryproject.com/about-us.html.

27. Histocrats homepage, http://histocrats.blogspot.com.

28. Welcome to the Georgian Lords blog series, https://thehistoryof-parliament.wordpress.com/the-georgian-lords/.

29. P.W. Singer and Emerson Brooking, "The Little-Known Story of Donald Trump's First Tweet," *TIME*, October 2, 2018, https://time.com/5412016/donald-trump-realdonaldtrump-twitter-first-tweet.

30. Andrew Chadwick, *The Hybrid Media System: Politics and Power*, Second Edition (Oxford: Oxford University Press, 2017), 255.

31. Chadwick, *Hybrid Media System*, 259.

32. Peter Gibbon, "Historians Disagree About Everything, or So It Seems" *HUMANITIES*, Summer 2017, Volume 38, Number 3, https://www.neh.gov/humanities/2017/summer/feature/historians-disagree-about-everything-or-so-it-seems.

33. Philip Scarpino and Daniel Vivian, "What Do Public History Employers Want? Report of the Joint AASLH-AHA-NCPH-OAH Task Force on Public History Education and Employment," published on the National Council of Public History website in February 2019, 10.

34. Study by the author of 1500 historians and History accounts on Twitter, conducted over a period from January 2019 to June 2020. Analysis of Twitter accounts done via Social Feed Manager, RStudio and Microsoft Excel.

35. Seth Cotlar (@SethCotlar), Twitter, August 15, 2019, https://twitter.com/SethCotlar/status/1162067597539438592.

36. William Horne, "Four Years of Doing Activist History," *The Activist History Review*, January 20, 2021, https://activisthistory.com/2021/01/20/four-years-of-doing-activist-history/.

37. Ren LaForme, "10 percent of Twitter users create 80 percent of tweets, study finds," *Poynter*, April 24, 2019, https://www.poynter.org/tech-tools/2019/10-percent-of-twitter-users-create-80-percent-of-all-tweets-study-finds/.

38. Emma Pettit, "How Kevin Kruse became history's attack dog," *The Chronicle of Higher Education*, December 16, 2018, https://www.chronicle.com/article/How-Kevin-Kruse-Became/245321.

39. Rebecca Onion, "Making History Go Viral," *Slate*, December 11, 2018, https://slate.com/news-and-politics/2018/12/twitter-history-viral-threads-2018.html.

40. See Beki Winchel, "Report: 83% of journalists use Twitter—but most still want email pitches," *PR Daily*, July 3, 2019, https://www.prdaily.com/report-83-of-journalists-use-twitter-but-most-still-want-email-pitches/ and Haje Jan Kamps, "25 percent of Twitter's verified users are journalists or media outlets," *Nieman Lab*, reposted from Medium, August 27, 2015, https://www.niemanlab.org/reading/25-percent-of-twitters-verified-users-are-journalists-or-media-outlets.

41. David S. Broder, "David Broder's decades of political insight, in his own words," *The Washington Post*, March 13, 2011.
42. See Edward Maibach, Roxanne Louiselle Parrott, eds., *Designing Health Messages: Approaches from Communication Theory and Public Health Practice*, (Thousand Oaks, CA: Sage Publications, 1995).
43. Chadwick, *The Hybrid Media System*, 23.
44. Chadwick, *The Hybrid Media System*, 23.
45. Chadwick, *The Hybrid Media System*, 254.
46. Mansoor Iqbal, "Instagram Revenue and Usage Statistics (2021)" Business of Apps, Updated: January 28, 2021, https://www.businessofapps.com/data/instagram-statistics/#1.

CHAPTER 6

1. Ian Gertler, "Internet Trends 2015 | Mary Meeker | KPCB," posted on slideshare.net, published May 27, 2015, slide 68, https://www.slideshare.net/iangertler/internet-trends-2015.
2. Uta Russman and Jakob Svensson,"Studying Organizations on Instagram," *Information*, 7 (4), 58 (2016), http://doi.org/10.3390/info7040058.
3. "Instagram by the Numbers: Stats, Demographics & Fun Facts," Omnicore, updated: January 6, 2021, https://www.omnicore-agency.com/instagram-statistics.
4. H.S. Hwang and J. Cho, "Why Instagram? Intention to continue using Instagram among Korean college students," *Social Behavior and Personality*, 46(8) (2018), 1305–1315. doi: http://dx.doi.org.ezp1.villanova.edu/10.2224/sbp.6961.
5. History Cool Kids (@historycoolkids), Instagram, https://www.instagram.com/historycoolkids/, accessed February 4, 2021.
6. History Cool Kids Patreon, https://www.patreon.com/history-coolkids, accessed February 4, 2021.
7. McKenzie Milhousen, "The coolest kid in history class," *Whalebone*, April 2019, https://whalebonemag.com/historycoolkids-interview/.
8. Milhousen, "The coolest kid in history class."
9. Lena De Casparis, "History Cool Kids—The New Instagram Account To Make You Weep," *Elle*. August 29, 2019, https://www.elle.com/uk/life-and-culture/culture/a28851445/historys-cool-kids-instagram/

10. "Historical Feeds (Almost) as Educational as The History Channel," *The GramList*, August 30, 2018, http://thegramlist.com/lists/historical-feeds/.

11. Milhousen, "The coolest kid in history class."

12. Conversation between the author and an international journalist, December 22, 2020.

13. Lene Hansen, "How images make world politics: International icons and the case of Abu Ghraib," *Review of International Studies*, Vol. 41, No. 2 (April 2015), 263–288.

14. Said founder Kevin Systrom, "We set out to solve the main problem with taking pictures on a mobile phone," he said, which is that they are often blurry or poorly composed. "We fixed that." See Jenna Wortham, "A Stream of Postcards, Shot by Phone," *The Ledger*, June 4, 2011.

15. Jenna Wortham, "A Stream of Postcards, Shot By Phone."

16. Jan-Ola Östman, "The postcard as media," *Interdisciplinary Journal for the Study of Discourse*, 24.3 (2004), http://kmdwiki.dmu.ac.uk/maphotohistory09_2/images/e/e3/Swproxy.pdf

17. Book event with Sarah Frier, author of *No Filter: The Untold Story of Instagram and How It Changed the Way We Live* (New York: Simon & Schuster, 2020), in the Human Behavior club on Clubhouse, October 9, 2020.

18. Kimberlee Morrison, "Why Instagram is a Ripe Opportunity for Brands," *Adweek*, August 20, 2015, https://www.adweek.com/digital/why-instagram-is-a-ripe-opportunity-for-brands-infographic/.

19. "Why Brands Should Embrace Instagram Instead of Facebook," Selfstartr, based on a work at ecommerceceo.com, https://selfstartr.com/why-brands-should-embrace-instagram-instead-of-facebook/.

20. Luis Vicente Casaló Ariño, Carlos Flavian and Sergio Ibáñez Sánchez, "Influencers on Instagram: Antecedents and consequences of opinion leadership," *Journal of Business Research*, July 2018, https://doi.org/10.1016/j.jbusres.2018.07.005.

21. Simon Owens, "Is It Time to Regulate Social Media Influencers?" *New York Magazine*, January 17, 2019. http://nymag.com/intelligencer/2019/01/is-it-time-to-regulate-social-media-influencers.html.

22. Hwang, and Cho, "Why Instagram?"

23. Guy Trebay, "Luka Sabbat, the 18-year-old fashion influencer," *The New York Times,* April 8, 2016, https://www.nytimes.com/2016/04/08/fashion/mens-style/luka-sabbat-fashion-influencer.html.
24. Casaló Ariño, Flavian and Sánchez, "Influencers on Instagram."
25. Yonatan T. Tewelde, "Seeing the image of an Eritrean Hero," *Journal of African Cultural Studies,* Vol. 27, No. 2 (June 2015), 172–180.
26. Leigh Raiford, "'Come Let Us Build a New World Together': SNCC and Photography of the Civil Rights Movement," *American Quarterly,* Dec. 2007, Vol. 59, No. 4 (Dec. 2007), 1129–1157.
27. As Harvard professor Steven Pinker wrote, "Few people are interested in how professors spend their time." See Steven Pinker, "Why Academics Stink at Writing," *The Chronicle of Higher Education,* September 26, 2014, https://www.chronicle.com/article/Why-Academics-Writing/148989.
28. Pinker, "Why Academics Stink at Writing."
29. Meghan Wright, "Why I don't use Instagram for science outreach," *Science,* March 15, 2018, https://www.sciencemag.org/careers/2018/03/why-i-dont-use-instagram-science-outreach.
30. Evan Goldstein, "The Academy is Responsible for its Own Peril," *Chronicle of Higher Education,* November 13, 2018, https://www.chronicle.com/article/The-Academy-Is-Largely/245080.
31. "Why We're Giving Up Conferences," Lady Science, published on January 6, 2019, https://www.ladyscience.com/ideas/why-were-giving-up-conferences-in-2019.
32. Lene Hansen, "How images make world politics: International icons and the case of Abu Ghraib" *Review of International Studies,* Vol. 41, No. 2 (April 2015), 263–288.
33. Raiford, "'Come Let Us Build a New World Together.'"
34. Brandy Zadrozny, "Twitter account that amplified Covington Catholic D.C. March video appears linked to California teacher," NBCNews.com, January 23, 2019, https://www.nbcnews.com/news/us-news/twitter-account-amplified-covington-catholic-d-c-march-video-appears-n961981.
35. Zadrozny, "Twitter account that amplified Covington Catholic D.C. March video."
36. See "Video of US teenagers taunting Native American draws fire," BBCNews, January 20, 2019, https://www.bbc.com/news/

world-us-canada-46935701 and Morgan Gstalter, "Haaland condemns students' behavior toward Native elder at Indigenous Peoples March" *The Hill*, January 19, 2019, https://thehill.com/blogs/blog-briefing-room/news/426160-haaland-condemns-students-behavior-toward-native-elder-at?.

37. Alice Marwick and Rebecca Lewis, "Media Manipulation and Disinformation Online," Data & Society Research Institute, https://datasociety.net/library/media-manipulation-and-disinfo-online/, 39.

38. LofiNikita (@lofinikita), Twitter, https://twitter.com/lofinikita/status/1086480504713445376, accessed January 24, 2019. Account no longer exists, tweet no longer accessible.

39. KatherineMariePrice (@KatiaPriceless), Twitter, https://twitter.com/KatiaPriceless/status/1086503334071205888; and IV Words (@IV_Words), Twitter, https://twitter.com/IV_Words/status/1086496648728072192; and Democracy Rocks! (@RocksDemocracy), Twitter, https://twitter.com/timm_emily/status/1086479292865892352. All accessed January 24, 2019.

40. Additional video footage posted online showed the incident to be far lengthier and more complicated than the short segment on Twitter suggested. The white students had, moments earlier, been confronted by Black Hebrew Israelites who called them "crackers," "peckerwoods" and "future school shooters." They responded by chanting The White Stripes song, "Seven Nation Army," in the process getting agitated and aggressive. The Native man told journalists he was attempting to intervene between the Israelites and the teens. Multiple indigenous activists and students filmed the incident, the activists with professional cameras and the students with their cell phones. In some footage, the students and activists can be seen clapping and dancing in unison. One person cries out confusedly, "What is going on?" See @SeedSovereignty, Twitter, https://twitter.com/SeedSovereignty/status/1086662362646466560.

41. Harry Callahan (@Harry_Callahan), Twitter, https://twitter.com/Harry_Callahan/status/1086524048790769664, accessed January 24, 2019.

42. TinEye search conducted March 7, 2021, search result page 21 out of 37, source website identified as http://www.imgrum.net/tag/selectednotelected and search result page 25 out of

37, source website identified as https://www.pinterest.de/pin/378724649903891455/.

43. Alonzo Smith, "The Omaha Courthouse Lynching of 1919," BlackPast.org, January 22, 2007, https://www.blackpast.org/african-american-history/omaha-courthouse-lynching-1919/.

44. File: Omaha courthouse lynching.jpg, Wikipedia, https://en.wikipedia.org/wiki/File:Omaha_courthouse_lynching.jpg.

45. TinEye search conducted March 7, 2021.

46. Term used by scholar Lene Hansen in her article, "How images make world politics: International icons and the case of Abu Ghraib" *Review of International Studies*, Vol. 41, No. 2 (April 2015), 263–288.

47. Barbara Waxer (@barbarawaxer), Twitter, https://twitter.com/barbarawaxer/status/1086505706298081280, accessed January 24, 2019.

48. Barbara Waxer, LinkedIn, https://www.linkedin.com/feed/update/urn:li:activity:6492802945372033024/, accessed January 24, 2019.

49. Barbara Waxer, LinkedIn.

50. See Barbara Waxer's personal website, "Applied Copyright: Find & Use Free Media," http://www.barbarawaxer.com/, accessed Sunday, March 14, 2021.

51. TinEye reverse image search, conducted Sunday, March 14, 2021, https://tineye.com/search/0378fbc3b0e811681e62b2b549bb06f5c51ff388?sort=crawl_date&order=asc&page=1.

52. Homepage of "We Shall Not Be Moved: The Jackson Woolworth's Sit-In and the Movement it Inspired," http://www.notbemoved.com/, accessed Sunday, March 14, 2021.

53. S. ZA, "Jackson, Mississippi. 1963," Iconic Photos: Famous, Infamous and Iconic Photos" website, January 19, 2015, https://iconicphotos.wordpress.com/2015/01/19/6085/.

54. Emily Wagster Pettus, "Anne Moody, sat stoically at violent Woolworth's sit-in, dies at 74," *Los Angeles Times*, February, 10, 2015, https://www.latimes.com/local/obituaries/la-me-anne-moody-20150211-story.html.

55. Sheena Goodyear, "Drowned Syrian boy photo joins long list of iconic news images," *CBC News*, September 4, 2015, https://www.cbc.ca/news/world/iconic-news-photos-1.3213945.

56. Alex Horton, "Before video of a Starbucks arrest, images of lunch counter sit-ins helped launch a movement," *The Washington Post*, April 17, 2018, https://www.washingtonpost.com/news/retropolis/wp/2018/04/17/before-video-of-a-starbucks-arrest-images-of-lunch-counter-sit-ins-helped-launch-a-movement/.

57. Lene Hansen, "How images make world politics: International icons and the case of Abu Ghraib" *Review of International Studies*, Vol. 41, No. 2 (April 2015), 263–288.

58. @mikeplugh, Twitter, January 19, 2019, https://twitter.com/OrangeandPloo/status/1086683823625195522/photo/1. Account suspended, tweet no longer accessible.

59. Christopher Mathias (@letsgomathias), Twitter, January 19, 2019, https://twitter.com/letsgomathias/status/1086673577934503936.

60. Lady Diana M (@LadyDianaM2), Twitter, January 19, 2019, https://twitter.com/LadyDianaM2/status/1086684868505784320.

61. Bob Andrews (@commishbob), Twitter, January 19, 2019, https://twitter.com/commishbob/status/1086773099566194689.

62. @RossTime, Twitter, January 19, 2019, https://twitter.com/RossTime/status/1086528146881548289. Accessed January 24, 2019, tweet deleted, account suspended.

63. Wellington wellsmitherson (@beautifulswamp), Twitter, January 19, 2019, https://twitter.com/florencehymns/status/1086653793012338688.

64. To What End—A quelle fin? (@ToWhatEnd1), Twitter, January 19, 2019, https://twitter.com/ToWhatEnd1/status/1086664434091732992.

65. Joanne Robrahn (@abynorml), Twitter, January 19, 2019, https://twitter.com/abynorml/status/1086761627389693953; and Glenna Hanna (@glennahanna), Twitter, January 19, 2019, https://twitter.com/glennhanna/status/1086769211374858240.

66. By Kate Conger and Sheera Frenkel, "Who Posted Viral Video of Covington Students and Protester? Congress Wants to Know," *New York Times*, January 23, 2019, https://www.nytimes.com/2019/01/23/technology/covington-video-protester-congress.html.

67. Zadrozny, "Twitter account that amplified Covington Catholic D.C. March video."

68. Arming Teachers (@ArmingTeachers), Twitter, captured by archive, today webpage capture, accessible at http://archive.is/0tJfo, accessed January 24, 2019.

69. user/ARREST_HILLARY_NOW/, "Trump supporters mocking an elder Native American at Indigenous People's March," r/politicalvideos, Reddit, https://www.reddit.com/r/PoliticalVideos/comments/ahjgt2/trump_supporters_mocking_an_elder_native_american.

70. u/MaDdBlaKkNews, "Guy with a MAGA hat mocking a elder Native American protestor" Reddit, https://www.reddit.com/user/MaDdBlaKkNews/comments/ahlezy/guy_with_a_maga_hat_mocking_a_elder_native.

71. u/gibson76, "Guy with a MAGA hat mocking a elder Native American protestor at Indigenous Peoples March" r/Fuckthealtright, Reddit, https://www.reddit.com/r/Fuckthealtright/comments/aho4c1/guy_with_a_maga_hat_mocking_a_elder_native.

72. See the original Instagram post by Ka_ya11, with caption: "More videos on YouTube: Kc Noland. The amount of disrespect... TO THIS DAY. #SMH #ipmdc19 #ipmdc #indigenousunited #indigenouspeoplesmarch #indigenouspeoplesmarch2019," posted January 18, 2019, https://www.instagram.com/p/Bsy80cfFVAR/.

73. Tiffany Ann Brown, "Reshaping Public Opinion Through Computational Propaganda," November 4, 2018, https://tiffanyabrown.wordpress.com.

74. Steve Andriole, "Mueller Was Right Again—This Time It's Russian Election Interference with Social Media," *Forbes*, October 11, 2019, https://www.forbes.com/sites/steveandriole/2019/10/11/mueller-was-right-again-this-time-its-russian-election-interference-with-social-media/#788f67b35405.

75. Mitch Chaiet, "Engineering Inflammatory Content: A Memetic Analysis of Russian Social Media Propaganda," Media Studies Thesis, The University of Texas at Austin, July 12, 2019.

76. Information from The Russia Tweets website, compiled and published by Professors Darren Linvill and Patrick Warren with FiveThirtyEight, a project of Defending Democracy Together, http://russiatweets.com.

77. Conversation between editor Andy Kifer and the author, January 2021.

CHAPTER 7

1. *USA Today* editor-in-chief Nicole Carroll told CNN's Brian Stelter in 2019 that social media had "changed everything—the speed that news travels, how we report the news, how we spread the news." See the CNN Reliable Sources newsletter, December 23, 2019. Upon her resignation from *The New York Times*, columnist Bari Weiss said that Twitter had become the *Times*'s "ultimate editor." See Bari Weiss resignation letter, https://www.bariweiss.com/resignation-letter, accessed February 19, 2021.
2. Nicole Hemmer, "How to Op-ed: Advice from @Pastpunditry (aka Nicole Hemmer)," History Communication website, June 1, 2017, https://historycommunication.com/2017/06/01/how-to-op-ed-advice-from-pastpunditry-aka-nicole-hemmer/.
3. Jim Rutenberg, "For News Outlets Squeezed From the Middle, It's Bend or Bust," *The New York Times*, April 17, 2016.
4. Rutenberg, "For News Outlets Squeezed From the Middle, It's Bend or Bust."
5. Philip M. Napoli, "Understanding our New Communications Economy: Implications for Contemporary Journalism," in Mark Lloyd, Lewis A. Friedland (eds.) *The Communication Crisis in America, And How to Fix It*, (New York: Palgrave MacMillan, 2016).
6. "#ConnectedGov: Partnership for Public Service," Booz Allen Hamilton social media, 2004.
7. Andrew Chadwick, *The Hybrid Media System: Politics and Power*, Second Edition (Oxford: Oxford University Press, 2017), 261.
8. Lucinda Southern, "Publishers are growing audiences by producing less content," *Digiday*, February 3, 2020, https://digiday.com/media/publishers-growing-audiences-producing-less-content/.
9. Amanda Meade, "News Corp tabloid the Herald Sun offers journalists cash bonuses for clicks," *The Guardian*, June 24, 2019.
10. Franklin Foer, *World Without Mind* (New York: Penguin, 2017).
11. Dustin Curtis, "Nick Denton's Crisis Letter to Gawker," December 10, 2014, https://dcurt.is/nick-denton-crisis-letter.
12. Thomas R. Schmidt, *Rewriting the Newspaper: The Storytelling Movement in American Print Journalism* (Columbia, MO: University of Missouri Press 2019), 103.

13. Bram De Ridder, "When the Analogy Breaks: Historical References in Flemish News Media at the Onset of the COVID-19 Pandemic," *Journal of Applied History* (2020) 1–16.

14. Nicole Hemmer, "How To Op-Ed: Advice From @Pastpunditry (Aka Nicole Hemmer)," History Communication website, June 1, 2017, https://historycommunication.com/2017/06/01/how-to-op-ed-advice-from-pastpunditry-aka-nicole-hemmer/.

15. Comment by Susan Reverby on Facebook, July 18, 2020, in response to a post by Nathaniel Comfort that shared her Medium article, "Now Do you Know Someone Sick or Dying from Covid 19?" Response from @Susan Reverby, "Very kind of you. Washington Post editorial person told me it was too historical when they rejected it."

16. Anecdote told to the author in March 2016.

17. Email from scholar Thomas R. Schmidt to the author, July 23, 2020.

18. See Schmidt, *Rewriting the Newspaper*. Schmidt's book chronicles the business challenges facing newspapers in far greater depth.

19. Napoli, "Understanding our New Communications Economy."

20. John Herrman, "Media Websites Battle Faltering Ad Revenue and Traffic," *The New York Times*. April 17, 2016.

21. Michael Posner, "Why Journalism Urgently Needs A Domestic Marshall Plan -- And Democracy Demands It," *Forbes*, February 7, 2019, https://www.forbes.com/sites/michaelposner/2019/02/07/why-journalism-urgently-needs-a-domestic-marshall-plan-and-democracy-demands-it/#7932c06067dd.

22. Morning Tech newsletter, *Politico*, Wednesday, June 26, 2019.

23. "1619 Project," New York Times Magazine, August 14, 2019, https://www.nytimes.com/interactive/2019/08/14/magazine/1619-america-slavery.html, accessed August 17, 2019.

24. "The Washington Post launches Made By History," The Washington Post, June 26, 2017, https://www.washingtonpost.com/pr/wp/2017/06/26/the-washington-post-launches-made-by-history.

25. "Current Events in Historical Perspective," *Perspectives on History: The Magazine of the American Historical Association*, https://www.historians.org/publications-and-directories/perspectives-on-history/current-events-in-historical-context.

26. Origins: A Project of the Departments of History of The Ohio State University and Miami University, https://origins.osu.edu/history-talk.

27. Mission Statement, History News Network, https://historynews-network.org/mission-statement.html.

28. History   Central,   https://www.historycentral.com/Relevanthistory.html.

29. "New American History" summary document, 2015.

30. Ralph Ellis, Ed Payne, Evan Perez and Dana Ford, "Shooting suspect in custody after Charleston church massacre," *CNN*, Updated 11:50 PM EDT, Thursday June 18, 2015, https://www.cnn.com/2015/06/18/us/charleston-south-carolina-shooting/index.html.

31. See Mother Jones, "Dylann Roof Authored a Horrifyingly Racist Manifesto," *Mother Jones*, June 20, 2015, https://www.motherjones.com/politics/2015/06/alleged-charleston-shooter-dylann-roof-manifesto-racist and; Clara Jeffery and James West, "The Deeply Racist References in Dylann Roof's Apparent Manifesto, Decoded," *Mother Jones*, June 20, 2015, https://www.motherjones.com/politics/2015/06/references-dylann-roof-manifesto-explained-1488/.

32. "Statement by the President on the Shooting in Charleston, South Carolina," The White House, June 18, 2015, https://obamawhitehouse.archives.gov/the-press-office/2015/06/18/statement-president-shooting-charleston-south-carolina.

33. Chadwick, *The Hybrid Media System*, 254.

34. Manisha Sinha, "The Long and Proud History of Charleston's AME Church," *HuffPost*, June 19, 2015, https://www.huffpost.com/entry/the-long-and-proud-history-of-charlestons-ame-church_b_7620910.

35. Yoni Appelbaum, "The Fight for Equality in Charleston, From Denmark Vesey to Clementa Pinckney," *The Atlantic*, June 18, 2015, https://www.theatlantic.com/politics/archive/2015/06/denmark-vesey-clementa-pinckney/396251/.

36. Jason Morgan Ward, "Dylann Roof and the white fear of a black takeover," *Chicago Tribune*, June 19, 2015, https://www.chicagotribune.com/nation-world/la-oe-0621-ward-charleston-ame-shooting-20150619-story.html

37. Emma Pettit, "For Historians, the Business of Studying Monuments Like UNC's Silent Sam Takes a Toll," *Chronicle of Higher Education*, August 21, 2018, https://www.chronicle.com/article/For-Historians-the-Business/244326?cid=cp220.

38. Pettit, "Business of Studying Monuments."

39. CBS Mornings, "Army Brigadier General Ty Seidule served his country for more than 30 years. His new book, "Robert E. Lee and Me" is a searing attack not just on his upbringing, but on some ugly parts of America that endure. @jeffglor has more:," Twitter, January 23, 2021, https://twitter.com/CBSThisMorning/status/1352963064220573696.

40. Dr. Ibram X. Kendi website, https://www.ibramxkendi.com/about and https://www.ibramxkendi.com/bio.

41. Email from a New York Times opinion editor to the author, July 29, 2020.

42. Peter J. Beck, *Presenting History: Past and Present* (Houndmills, Basingstoke, Hampshire; New York, NY: Palgrave Macmillan, 2012), 95.

43. Theresa L. Miller, Emilie L'Hôte and Andrew Volmert, *Communicating about History: Challenges, Opportunities, and Emerging Recommendations* (Washington, D.C.: FrameWorks Institute, 2020).

44. "Kevin Kruse" contributor page, MSNBC, https://www.msnbc.com/author/kevin-m-kruse-ncpn1243097, accessed February 17, 2021.

45. Miller, L'Hôte, and Volmert, *Communicating about History*.

46. This was taught to me by Emeritus Historian of the U.S. Senate Don Ritchie.

47. These include Michael Beschloss, Doris Kearns Goodwin, Jon Meacham, David McCullough and Jacob Weisberg. It's worth noting that each are white and attended elite Northeastern universities: Isaacson (Harvard); Burns (Hampshire College); McCullogh (Yale); Kearns Goodwin (Harvard); Beschloss (Harvard).

48. See Karin Wulf, "What Naomi Wolf and Cokie Roberts teach us about the need for historians," *The Washington Post*, June 11, 2019, https://www.washingtonpost.com/outlook/2019/06/11/what-naomi-wolf-cokie-roberts-teach-us-about-need-historians.

49. History is not the first discipline that journalists have appropriated. Starting in the 1960s and into the 1990s, adherents to New

Journalism claimed to be sociologists and anthropologists. See Schmidt, *Rewriting the Newspaper*, 98.

50. Corey Robin, "Why Has it Taken Us So Long to See Trump's Weaknesses?" *New York Magazine*, February 20, 2019. http://nymag.com/intelligencer/2019/02/corey-robin-on-the-historovox-what-we-missed-about-trump.html.

51. About page, Nikole Hannah Jones website, https://nikolehannahjones.com/about/.

52. See Sean Wilentz, "A Matter of Facts," *The Atlantic*, January 22, 2020, https://www.theatlantic.com/ideas/archive/2020/01/1619-project-new-york-times-wilentz/605152/.

53. Homepage, "Project 1619" website, https://www.project1619.org, accessed August 1, 2021.

54. According to her talent agency bio, Hannah-Jones holds a BA in History and African-American Studies. This again raises the question of how much history education one needs in order to be recognized as a professional historian. See Nikole Hannah-Jones, the Lavin Agency, https://www.thelavinagency.com/speakers/nikole-hannah-jones, accessed August 3, 2021.

55. Karine Nahon and Jeff Hemsley, *Going Viral* (Cambridge, UK: Polity Press, 2013), 72.

56. Jason Koebler, Anna Merlan and Joseph Cox, "Silicon Valley Elite Discuss Journalists Having Too Much Power in Private App," Motherboard Tech By *Vice*, July 2, 2020, https://www.vice.com/en_us/article/n7w3zw/silicon-valley-elite-discuss-journalists-having-too-much-power-in-private-app.

57. "Podcasting Market Size, Share & Trends Analysis Report By Genre (News & Politics, Society & Culture, Comedy, Sports), By Formats (Interviews, Panels, Solo), And Segment Forecasts, 2020–2027," Grand View Research, August 2020, https://www.grandviewresearch.com/industry-analysis/podcast-market.

CHAPTER 8

1. From the podcast "H101, Conversational history with a focus on narrative," http://www.hi101.ca/, accessed January 19, 2021.

2. iTunes search for history podcasts by the author, January 2020.

3. Ali Tobey, "'Stuff You Missed In History Class' brings history out of textbooks," *Maine Campus,* April 1, 2019, https://mainecampus.com/2019/04/stuff-you-missed-in-history-class-brings-history-out-of-textbooks.

4. History That Doesn't Suck! website, https://historythatdoesntsuck.com/about, accessed January 20, 2021.

5. History Impossible website, https://www.historyimpossible.com, accessed January 20, 2021.

6. Tobey, "Stuff You Missed In History Class."

7. One Mic: Black History, https://www.onemichistory.com/, accessed August 1, 2021.

8. The Washington Post, "Retropod," https://www.washingtonpost.com/podcasts/retropod/, accessed August 1, 2021.

9. Conversation with the author, December 31, 2020.

10. "Podcasting Market Size, Share & Trends Analysis Report By Genre (News & Politics, Society & Culture, Comedy, Sports, Repurposed Content), By Formats (Interviews, Panels, Solo, Conversational), And Segment Forecasts, 2020–2027", Grand View Research, August 2021, https://www.grandviewresearch.com/industry-analysis/podcast-market#:~:text=Report%20Overview,27.5%25%20from%202020%20to%202027.

11. Spotify Sustainability and Social Impact Report, 2019.

12. Spotify Sustainability and Social Impact Report, 2019.

13. Nicholas Quah, "Vice is bringing in a big audio team to do new kinds of podcasts—from a daily news show to a seasonal series," *Nieman Lab,* August 18, 2020, https://www.niemanlab.org/2020/08/vice-is-bringing-in-a-big-audio-team-to-do-new-kinds-of-podcasts-from-a-daily-news-show-to-a-seasonal-series.

14. Contributor, "Lessons from award-winning podcasts: History Extra Podcast's Dave Musgrove," *What's New in Publishing | Digital Publishing News,* April 23, 2020, https://whatsnewinpublishing.com/lessons-from-award-winning-podcasts-history-extra-podcasts-dave-musgrove.

15. This transformation is detailed in Thomas R. Schmidt's book *Rewriting the Newspaper: The Storytelling Movement in American Print Journalism* (Columbia, MO: University of Missouri Press, 2019), as well as the book summary on Google Scholar: https://scholar.google.com/citations?view_op=view_citation&hl=en&use

r=5DoADN8AAAAJ&citation_for_view=5DoADN8AAAAJ:U
eHWp8X0CEIC.

16. Alyssa Schukar, "Pete Buttigieg's Focus: Storytelling First. Policy Details Later," *The New York Times*, April 14, 2019, https://www.nytimes.com/2019/04/14/us/politics/pete-buttigieg-2020-writing-message.html.

17. Brianne Carlon Rush, "Science of storytelling: why and how to use it in your marketing," *The Guardian*, August 28, 2014, https://www.theguardian.com/media-network/media-network-blog/2014/aug/28/science-storytelling-digital-marketing.

18. Conversation on Clubhouse, January 17, 2021.

19. Conversation with the author, October 30, 2020.

20. Statistics tweeted by historian Julie Golia during the 2016 American Historical Association annual meeting, session s161, "Podcasting History: A Roundtable Discussion," January 9, 2016, https://storify.com/JulieG1210/tweeting-aha-session-161-podcasting-history. Storify no longer accessible.

21. Julie Golia (@JulieThePH), Twitter, re: Betsy Beasley at the 2016 American Historical Association annual meeting.

22. Description found on the Apple Podcasts page for "Now & Then," https://podcasts.apple.com/us/podcast/introducing-now-then/id1567665859?i=1000521770053, accessed July 18, 2021.

23. Alex V. Cipolle, "Q&A with Hardcore History's Dan Carlin: Print Edition," EugeneWeekly.com, December 24, 2014, accessed via the Internet Archive Wayback Machine, https://web.archive.org/web/20180127025222/http://www.eugeneweekly.com/20141224/culture/qa-hardcore-history%E2%80%99s-dan-carlin.

24. Conversation on Clubhouse, September 14, 2020.

25. Eric Johnson, "Malcolm Gladwell wants his new podcast to make you cry," *Vox*, June 16, 2016, https://www.vox.com/2016/6/16/11934370/malcolm-gladwell-podcast-revisionist-history-mass-shootings.

26. Miranda Sawyer, "The week in radio: Revisionist History; Beautiful Stories from Anonymous People," *The Guardian*, August 21, 2016, https://www.theguardian.com/tv-and-radio/2016/aug/21/the-week-in-radio-revisionist-history-beautiful-stories-from-anonymous-people-podcast.

27. 1A WAMU, "All Talk, Political Action: How Conservative Talk Radio Shaped The GOP," National Public Radio, August 12, 2019, https://the1a.org/segments/2019-08-12-conservative-talk-radio/.

28. Melissa A. Johnson, Keon M. Pettiway, "Visual Expressions of Black Identity: African American and African Museum Websites," *Journal of Communication*, Volume 67, Issue 3, June 2017, 350–377, https://doi.org/10.1111/jcom.12298.

29. Based on notes taken by the author from numerous presentations during the 11th International Conference on Social Media & Society, held online from July 22-24, 2020, https://socialmediaandsociety.org/.

30. Focus-group conversation held via Zoom on January 14, 2021.

31. Statistics from podcaster Espree Devora on Clubhouse, October 5, 2020.

32. Jeremiah Owyang, "The Future of Social Audio: Startups, Roadmap, Business Models, and a Forecast," Jeremiah Owyang website, January 30, 2021, https://web-strategist.com/blog/2021/01/30/the-future-of-social-audio-startups-roadmap-business-models-and-a-forecast.

33. See "History is About Stories. Here's Why We Get Them Wrong," TIME.com, https://time.com/5418740/history-neuroscience/ and Cryssa Bazos, "History is Storytelling," cryssabazos.com, February. 19, 2015, https://cryssabazos.com/2015/02/19/history-is-storytelling. See also Hayley R. Bowman, "What Story Do You Want to Tell?: Learning Narrative Storytelling through Podcasting" *Perspectives on History: the Newsmagazine of the American Historical Association*, July 8, 2021, https://www.historians.org/publications-and-directories/perspectives-on-history/summer-2021/what-story-do-you-want-to-tell-learning-narrative-storytelling-through-podcasting.

34. Conversation on Clubhouse, October 17, 2020.

35. Conversation on Clubhouse, October 17, 2020.

CHAPTER 9

1. Joseph Mah LinkedIn page, https://www.linkedin.com/in/joseph-mah-51399848, accessed July 25, 2021.

2. Robert Booth, "Unilever saves on recruiters by using AI to assess job interviews," *The Guardian*, October 25, 2019. https://www.theguardian.com/technology/2019/oct/25/unilever-saves-on-recruiters-by-using-ai-to-assess-job-interviews

3. "Alicia Kelso, "Here's Why Taco Bell Added Artificial Intelligence Technology To Its Mobile App," *Forbes*, January 23, 2020, https://www.forbes.com/sites/aliciakelso/2020/01/23/heres-why-taco-bell-added-artificial-intelligence-technology-to-its-mobile-app/?sh=205dde11d877.

4. "Deep Dive: Artificial Intelligence on the Rise," Aspen Ideas Festival, video presentation, https://www.aspenideas.org/sessions/deep-dive-artificial-intelligence-on-the-rise.

5. Tom Simonite, "Give These Apps Some Notes and They'll Write Emails for You," *WIRED*, October 18, 2020, https://www.wired.com/story/give-apps-notes-they-write-emails/.

6. OpenAI, "Solving Rubik's Cube with a Robot Hand," October 15, 2019, https://openai.com/blog/solving-rubiks-cube/.

7. Kevin Kelly, *The Inevitable: Understanding the 12 Technological Forces That Will Shape Our Future* (New York: Penguin, 2017).

8. Conversation between the author and a friend, December 31, 2020.

9. Query for "Who Discovered America" on SenseBot.com, retrieving 20 sentences from 6 sources, January 17, 2021.

10. Google's Chief of Staff for Health, Research & Innovation Lizzie Dorfman stated in 2019: "Artificial general intelligence would refer to a computer that can perform any possible human cognitive task at present and for the extended unforeseeable future. This is the stuff of science fiction. We are not remotely close to achieving that level of AI." See: "Deep Dive: Artificial Intelligence on the Rise," Aspen Ideas Festival, video presentation, https://www.aspenideas.org/sessions/deep-dive-artificial-intelligence-on-the-rise.

11. In a conversation on the social media app Clubhouse in August 2020, a manager at Google AI suggested that AGI is 5–20 years away.

12. Statistics taken from "Prof, no one is reading you," *The Strait Times*, April 11, 2015, accessed June 2, 2015. http://www.straitstimes.com/news/opinion/more-opinion-stories/story/prof-no-one-reading-you-20150411.

13. Sarah Kreps and Miles McCain, "Not Your Father's Bots," *Foreign Affairs*, August 2, 2019, https://www.foreignaffairs.com/articles/2019-08-02/not-your-fathers-bots.

14. Simon Smith, "Synthetic Journal Articles Could Drive Real Research Progress," *Wiley*, May 7, 2019, https://www.wiley.com/network/latest-content/synthetic-journal-articles-could-drive-real-research-progress.

15. Karen Hao, "A college-kid's fake, AI generated blog fooled tens of thousands. This is how he made it." *MIT Technology Review*, August 14, 2020, https://www.technologyreview.com/2020/08/14/1006780/ai-gpt-3-fake-blog-reached-top-of-hacker-news/.

16. N. Brown and T. Sandholm, "Superhuman AI for multiplayer poker," *Science*, (2019) https://doi.org/10.1126/science.aay2400.

17. As stated during a conversation on the social media app Clubhouse in August 2020.

18. See Claudio Demartini and Lorenzo Benussi, "Do Web 4.0 and Industry 4.0 Imply Education X.0?" *IT Pro*, published by the IEEE Computer Society, May/June 2017.

19. As reported by WIRED in 2019, a joint MIT and IBM study found that tasks that could be performed by AI were gradually disappearing from job listings and being replaced by soft skills. As a result, job openings for lower-income and higher-income positions were increasing, and job openings for middle-income professions were decreasing. See Sara Harrison, "AI May Not Kill Your Job—Just Change It," *WIRED*, October 31, 2019, https://www.wired.com/story/ai-not-kill-job-change-it/.

20. Langdon Winner, "Do Artifacts Have Politics?" *Daedalus*, Vol. 109, No. 1, Modern Technology: Problem or Opportunity? (Winter, 1980), 121–136.

21. Amir Rosic, "Blockchain for Beginners: What is Blockchain Technology? A Step-by-Step Guide," *Blockgeeks*, https://blockgeeks.com/guides/what-is-blockchain-technology/, accessed January 16, 2021.

22. Conversation with the author, January 13, 2021.

23. For details on how this operates on the Ethereum blockchain, see Proof of Beauty, "Into the $HASH-verse" published June 15, 2021, https://pob.mirror.xyz/3Os_kduyxwC9hjqCDjV4LMPKZ-4RrkYW64m5i5iYNcc; Proof of Beauty "Introducing Historians

DAO," published July 4, 2021, https://pob.mirror.xyz/viCa_nhTUcCuu5kqBhtlLK6JG3o_n5oKi3cODvKaN-8; and Proof of Beauty "Historians DAO," https://hash.pob.studio/historians. All accessed on July 25, 2021.

CHAPTER 10

1. Ella Ceron, "Social Media Star Essena O'Neill Shares a Tearful Thank You After Her Eye-Opening Instagram Posts Go Viral," *Teen Vogue*, November 3, 2015, https://www.teenvogue.com/story/essena-oneill-instagram-selfies-backstory.
2. Toward the end of researching this book, I discovered that Tim Wu also cited this Essena O'Neill anecdote in his book *Attention Merchants*—only from a different news source. It occurred to me that the story of Essena O'Neill quitting Instagram was, itself, an engineered product, replete with compelling media logic (beautiful woman gives up everything) and, perhaps, planted by O'Neill herself.
3. Essena O'Neill website, "Authority Within," accessed June 7, 2020, https://www.authoritywithin.com. YouTube channel statistics recorded by the author on January 17, 2021.
4. Alyx Gorman, "From sponsors to socialism: the return of Instagram star Essena O'Neill," *The Guardian*, November 19, 2019, https://www.theguardian.com/lifeandstyle/2019/nov/19/sponsors-socialism-return-instagram-star-essena-oneill.
5. Benjamin M. Schmidt, "The History BA since the Great Recession: The 2018 AHA Majors Report," American Historical Association, November 26, 2018, https://www.historians.org/publications-and-directories/perspectives-on-history/december-2018/the-history-ba-since-the-great-recession-the-2018-aha-majors-report.
6. Dylan Ruediger, "The 2021 AHA Jobs Report," American Historical Association, January 20, 2021, https://www.historians.org/ahajobsreport2021.
7. Conversation with the author on October 21, 2020.
8. Conversation on Clubhouse, December 15, 2020.
9. Rachel Boyle, "Still Grinding? How the pandemic is accelerating job precarity in public history," *History@Work*, March 11, 2021,

https://ncph.org/history-at-work/how-the-pandemic-is-accelerating-job-precarity-in-public-history.

10. Jerry Useem, "The Navy's USS Gabrielle Giffords and the Future of Work," *The Atlantic,* July 2019.

11. Leon Botstein, "Are We Still Making Citizens?" *Democracy: A Journal of Ideas*, No. 36 (Spring 2015), https://democracyjournal.org/magazine/36/are-we-still-making-citizens.

12. Cequea's animation about the history of systemic racism went viral on Facebook in June 2020. Tara Jaye Frank booked lucrative speaking deals with companies such as American Express with a talk titled, "Race in America: How Did We Get Here?"

13. Dane Kennedy, *The Imperial History Wars: Debating the British Empire*, (London: Bloomsbury, 2018), 20.

14. Josh Eidelson, "The Gig Economy Is Coming for Millions of American Jobs," *Bloomberg*, February 17, 2021, https://www.bloomberg.com/news/features/2021-02-17/gig-economy-coming-for-millions-of-u-s-jobs-after-california-s-uber-lyft-vote.

15. See Dylan Ruediger, "The 2021 AHA Jobs Report," American Historical Association, January 20, 2021, https://www.historians.org/ahajobsreport2021 for the employment situation in academia, and a public history Joint Task Force on Public History Education and Employment whose results are published at https://ncph.org/history-at-work/tag/joint-task-force.

16. See NASA Science for an overview of dark energy and dark matter, NASA Science, "Dark Energy, Dark Matter," NASA.gov, https://science.nasa.gov/astrophysics/focus-areas/what-is-dark-energy, accessed February 9, 2021. Sam Wineburg made a similar argument about the familiar past and the past whose applicability to the present was not immediately obvious in a 1999 article in the scholarly journal *Phi Delta Kappan*. See Sam Wineburg, "Historical Thinking and Other Unnatural Acts," *The Phi Delta Kappan*, Vol. 80, No. 7 (March, 1999), 488–499.

17. Bram De Ridder, "When the Analogy Breaks: Historical References in Flemish News Media at the Onset of the COVID-19 Pandemic," *Journal of Applied History* (2020), 1–16.

18. Isabella Avila @onlyjayus, "History Facts School Refuses to Teach You," video posted on TikTok, https://vm.tiktok.com/ZMJDrBhnr, accessed January 16, 2021.

19. John Backus, Chris Beiser and Byrne Hobart, "US History that sounds fake but isn't!" event hosted on Clubhouse, September 17, 2020.
20. Jill Lepore, "The Party Crashers," *The New Yorker*, February 22, 2016.
21. Langdon Winner, "Do Artifacts Have Politics?" *Daedalus*, Vol. 109, No. 1, Modern Technology: Problem or Opportunity? (Winter, 1980), 121–136.
22. Eric Berger, "American kids would much rather be YouTubers than astronauts," *Ars Technica*, July 16, 2019, https://arstechnica.com/science/2019/07/american-kids-would-much-rather-be-youtubers-than-astronauts/.

INDEX[1]

NUMBERS AND SYMBOLS
#Resistance, 51, 54
/r/HistoryPodcast, 88
/r/OldSchoolCool, 36
/r/ThisDayInHistory, 36

A
Academia/academics, 2, 5, 15, 23, 24,
    28, 30, 39, 52, 53, 63, 78, 80, 82,
    83, 85, 101, 105, 108, 110,
    111, 113
Activism, 28, 39, 82
Ads/advertising, 11, 22, 37, 38, 43,
    48, 60, 70, 74, 82, 84, 85
African Americans/African American
    History/Black History, 4, 70, 88
Amazon/Amazon Alexa, 24, 100,
    101, 113
America, 2, 39, 63, 66, 69–71, 78–80,
    110, 113

American Historical Association, 64, 83
Arnold, John, 14, 22, 25
Artificial Intelligence (A.I.), 6, 14, 17,
    99–107, 112, 113, 150
Atlantic, The, 28, 43, 49, 79, 80,
    102, 110
Australia, 43, 47, 49

B
BBC, 88, 89
Belgium, 75, 115
Berners-Lee, Tim, 19
Black Lives Matter, 7
Blockchain, 104, 105, 107,
    109, 111–113
Blog, 2, 21, 49, 63, 84
Boym, Svetlana, 37, 40
Brexit, 7
Burns, Ken, 80, 145
Buzzfeed, 13, 74

[1] Note: Page numbers followed by 'n' refer to notes.

C

Cambridge Analytica, 38
Cameron, Kyle, 43, 47, 58
Cannon, Carl M., 37
Carlin, Dan, 88, 92, 111
Carlos, John, 39
Cash, Johnny, 47
CERN, 19
Chadwick, Andrew, 53, 115
Charleston, 3, 78, 79
China, 38, 50
Chris "Wolfgang" Wild, 46, 48
Civil Rights/Civil Rights
    movement, 39, 40, 52,
    61, 65–67, 70, 81
Civil War, 1, 2, 4, 9, 13, 30, 54,
    57, 79–81
Classroom, 5, 7, 8, 15, 96, 103
Clinton, Hillary, 50
Clubhouse, 11, 87, 96, 107, 109,
    111, 115
CNN, 44, 71, 80, 81, 83, 84, 142
Colleges, 2, 3, 5, 25, 29, 101, 109,
    110, 112
Columbia University, 33
Confederate/confederacy, 4, 7, 69,
    71, 78–80
Conservatives, 1, 2, 25, 27, 45,
    50–53, 120n6
Conspiracies/conspiracy theorists,
    2, 28, 50
COVID-19, 75, 115
Crash Course, 5, 14, 15, 123
Credentials/credentialism,
    11, 21, 34, 82, 92,
    103–105, 109–111
Crowd-source/crowd-sourcing, 6, 17,
    19–31, 71, 105, 107, 111,
    112, 114
Crunchbase, 47
Cunningham, Ward, 21, 28, 58
Curator(s), 9, 62, 95, 113, 117

D

Data, 11, 12, 34–36, 38, 39, 74, 75,
    100–103, 113
Davison, Paul, 11
Decentralized Autonomous
    Organization (DAO), 105
Di Petta, Xavier, 43, 46, 47, 49, 58
Disinformation, 2, 4, 13, 14, 54,
    65, 66, 70
Disrupted/disruption, 3, 5, 7,
    21, 53, 109
Domby, Adam, 79, 80
D'Souza, Dinesh, 52, 111
Duterte, Rodrigo, 39

E

Eckford, Elizabeth, 68
Education, 5, 10, 14, 15, 58, 82, 103,
    109, 111–114
e-History, 1–17, 19, 20, 22, 24–28,
    30, 31, 33–41, 43, 44, 47, 48,
    50, 51, 53–55, 58–62, 64, 67,
    70, 71, 73–77, 80, 82, 85,
    87–90, 93, 94, 96, 97, 99–101,
    103, 105, 107–110, 113–117
Emancipation Proclamation, 2
Encyclopedia Britannica, 21
Enrollments, 5, 15, 38, 48, 80, 109, 114
Erdogan, Recep Tayyip, 38
Ethereum, 105
Exhibit/exhibitions, 9, 10, 16
Experts/expertise, 6, 9, 11, 12, 14, 15,
    20–25, 28–30, 33, 35, 43, 47, 48,
    58, 71, 74, 77–79, 82–84, 87, 89,
    94–97, 105, 109–112, 116

F

Facebook, 1, 4, 11, 12, 31, 33–40,
    43–45, 48, 57–60, 64, 70, 73,
    75, 76, 79, 87, 89, 111

Fake history, 115
Fake news, 82
Federal Trade Commission, 60
Feeds, 12, 13, 16, 17, 28, 29,
    33, 35, 36, 39, 52, 54,
    58–62, 71, 74, 75, 96,
    102, 103, 108
Foote, Shelby, 80
Foreign Affairs, 30, 102
Foreign Policy Research Institute, 29
4chan, 28, 67
Foursquare, 34
Frameworks Institute, 2, 15
Friendslist, 33, 34

G
Gawker, 75
Generation Z, 28
Gladwell, Malcolm, 88, 93
Google, 5, 11, 12, 35, 73, 76, 90,
    100, 102, 113
GPT-2, 102
GPT-3, 102
Green, John, 15
Guardian, The, 74, 79, 93

H
Hannah-Jones, Nikole, 83, 84, 146
Hardcore History, 5, 88, 92
Harvard, 62, 63, 82
Haymarket riots, 24
Hemmer, Nicole, 74, 75
Hemsley, Jeff, 7, 23, 45, 84
High school, 2, 14, 28, 29, 58, 68,
    101, 109
Historiography, 14, 74
Historovox, 82
History, 1, 9–17, 19, 33, 46, 58, 73,
    87, 99–117
HISTORY Channel, 13

History communication/history
    communicators, 5, 11, 24, 36,
    48, 53, 54, 61, 62, 71, 77, 92,
    95, 103, 112, 113, 116, 117
History Communication Institute, 112
History Cool Kids, 57, 58, 60, 62,
    82, 88, 107
HistoryinPics, 43–52, 54, 57, 58, 82,
    83, 88, 92, 93, 107, 111, 114
Humanities, 87, 89, 90, 110, 114
Hyperlinks, 3, 16, 20, 90

I
Ibrahim, Yasmin, 38
Indigenous/Native American, 65, 66,
    69, 81, 138
Influencers, 60, 63
Instagram, 1, 2, 5, 11, 29, 34, 37, 55,
    57–65, 68–70, 92, 105, 107,
    108, 110, 111
Internet, 5, 19, 20, 39, 48,
    49, 96, 116
Internet Research Agency, 70
Iran, 50
Isaacson, Walter, 20, 145

J
Japan, 27
Jinping, Xi, 38
Journalism/journalists, 2, 3, 5–7, 14,
    23, 25, 28–30, 34, 36, 37, 40,
    49, 51–53, 58, 62, 64, 66, 67,
    70, 74–78, 80–85, 89, 90, 92,
    101, 104, 107, 109, 112, 113,
    133, 138

K
Kendi, Ibram, 80
Khan Academy, 14, 15, 123

Korea (North Korea, South
    Korea), 27, 28
Kruse, Kevin, 52, 54, 81, 83, 120

L
League, Ivy, 52, 82
Lecture, 5, 13, 14, 16, 48, 58,
    87, 88, 111
Lee, Dain, 57, 58
Lepore, Jill, 63, 64, 116
Lewis, John, 39
Library of Congress, 20, 24, 25
Lincoln, Abraham, 2, 34, 40, 47, 65

M
Made by History, 77, 78, 84, 85
Make America Great Again, 38, 39, 65
Market logic, 12
Martin Luther King, Jr., 39, 65, 70
Memento, 36
MemoLane, 36, 48
Messer-Kruse, Timothy, 24, 25, 27, 29
Misinformation, 4, 23, 65, 109
Modi, Narenda, 38
Monuments, 7, 71, 79, 80
Mumford, Lewis, 13
Museum, 5, 8–10, 16, 36, 40, 48, 50,
    95, 104, 105, 112, 113, 116,
    117, 121
MyHeritage, 40

N
NAACP, 67, 78, 79
Nahon, Karine, 7, 23, 45, 84
National parks, 9, 40
Nazis/Nazism, 68
Netto uyoku, 27, 28, 105
The New Republic, 74
News feed, 3, 4, 35, 37–39, 44

News/news media, 1, 2, 4, 12, 13, 24,
    25, 29, 49, 52–54, 66, 71,
    73–77, 79–85, 89–91, 99, 102,
    105, 108, 109, 115
Networks, 12, 36, 43, 45, 59, 83, 84,
    92, 95, 100, 104, 111, 112, 117
New York, 3, 26, 27, 49
New York Times, 5, 71, 74, 77, 80, 81,
    83–85, 102
Nichols, Tom, 30
Non-Fungible Token (NFT), 105
North Carolina, 78, 79
Nostalgia, 6, 8, 17, 31, 33–41,
    43, 87, 107
NPR, 58, 88, 89, 101, 102
Nupedia, 21–23, 85

O
Obama, Barack, 44, 50, 61, 67, 78
The Oklahoman, 49
O'Neill, Essena, 108, 116, 152
"On This Day" (#OTD), 34, 36, 37,
    41, 83, 89
Open Source, 23
Orban, Viktor, 38
Oxford Dictionary, 35

P
Parade, 13, 122n15
Pakistan, 104
PhDs, 10, 11, 21, 109, 113, 121
Philippines, 39
Photography, 61, 65, 67
Pinterest, 67
Platforms, 3, 4, 6, 7, 11–13, 16, 19,
    20, 23, 27–30, 33, 36, 37, 40,
    41, 44, 45, 48, 49, 51–53,
    57–60, 62, 64, 76, 79, 84, 87,
    88, 96, 101, 103, 107, 108,
    111, 115–117

Podcast, 1, 2, 7, 37, 84, 85, 87–97, 99, 107, 110
Politico, 74, 84
PragerU, 1, 2, 4, 8, 14, 52, 54, 78
Presidential Historian, 81
Princeton, 52, 81, 82, 120
Progressives, 2, 15, 51, 53, 54, 65, 66, 68, 78, 120
Protest, 29, 65
Public history, 95, 111
Putin, Vladimir, 38

Q
Quora, 28, 102

R
Rebecca Onion, 132n17, 133n20, 133n21, 134n39
Reddit, 11, 12, 28, 41, 48, 65, 67, 68, 70, 73, 79, 102
Republicans/Republican Party, 2, 50–52
Retronaut, 44, 46, 48–50, 88, 93, 132, 133
Retropolis, 77
Richardson, Heather Cox, 52, 54, 91
Roberts, Kokie, 82
Roof, Dylann, 3, 78
Rosenzweig, Roy, 23, 27
Russia, 38
Russia Today, 5, 108

S
Sanger, Larry, 21, 22
Satisficing, 7, 23, 64
Science communicator/science communication, 63
Science Sam, 63, 64
Seidule, Ty, 1, 3, 4, 78–80

Selfie, 35, 39, 46
Silicon Valley, 3, 5, 11, 15, 44, 49, 81, 96, 113
Sinatra, Frank, 47
1619 Project, 77, 83
Slate, 52, 88
Smith, Tommie, 39
Snowzilla, 25–28, 62
Social media, 2, 5, 9, 12, 25, 35, 36, 38, 39, 43–46, 50, 52, 53, 59, 64, 65, 68, 70, 71, 73–75, 79, 81–84, 87, 95, 96, 108, 111, 112, 114–117
Social networks, 1, 4, 6, 35, 44, 45, 48, 57, 59, 96
Social Web, 1–6, 8, 9, 11–13, 15–17, 19–23, 26–28, 30, 33, 38–40, 43, 44, 47–50, 52, 54, 57, 59, 64, 65, 71, 73–75, 78, 82, 85, 87, 89–92, 95, 96, 107, 109–111, 115, 116
Society of the History Textbook Reform, 27
South Carolina, 3, 78
Spotify, 89, 92
Storytelling, 6, 12, 17, 85, 87–97, 107
Students, 2, 3, 6, 9, 10, 14, 15, 23, 25, 28, 29, 43, 51, 57, 58, 65, 68, 81, 88, 101, 103, 109, 112, 138
Syllabus, 16

T
Tabloids, 74
Teachers, 2, 14, 29, 50, 58, 68, 93, 107
TechCrunch, 34, 36, 37
Technology, 3, 5, 24, 37, 96, 102–104, 109, 112, 113, 116
TED/TEDx, 46, 47
Television, 7, 76, 90, 92, 95, 100

Textbook(s), 16, 28, 47, 58, 102, 117
"This Day in History" (#TDiH), 36
TikTok, 3, 11, 107, 111, 115
Timehop, 33–40, 43, 45, 47, 48, 77, 130
TIME magazine, 20, 77, 84, 85
Trump, Donald, 7, 38, 39, 45, 50–54, 57, 65–67, 84, 111
Tubman, Harriet, 39
Twitter, 1, 2, 5, 11, 12, 15, 34–37, 41, 43–55, 57, 58, 62, 64–66, 68–70, 73, 78, 79, 87, 95, 96, 99, 105, 107, 111
Twitterstorians, 51, 71
2chan, 27, 28
2020Fight, 65–68

U

University, 1, 5, 80, 82, 83, 90, 103, 116, 145
University presses/university publishing, 105
U.S. Army, 1, 4
Useem, Jerry, 110
Users, 3, 5, 7, 11–13, 15–17, 19–23, 25, 28, 29, 31, 33–40, 45–48, 51, 53, 55, 57–66, 68–71, 81, 89, 95, 96, 103–105, 107

V

Venture capital/venture capitalists, 16, 57, 96
Video, 1–4, 8, 14, 15, 20, 24, 37, 40, 44, 54, 65–68, 70, 78, 79, 96, 99, 107, 108, 110, 112, 115–117, 119, 138
Virality, 1, 2, 12, 43–47, 49, 50, 52, 53, 66, 71, 107

W

Wales, Jimmy, 11, 21, 22, 28, 29, 58
War, 2, 4, 9, 27, 40, 52, 54, 61, 66, 71, 92
Washington, D.C., 27, 44, 65, 70
Washington Post, 71, 76–78, 83–85, 88, 102
Web 1.0, 20
Web 2.0, 6, 11, 12, 19, 21, 30, 35, 73, 76, 90
Web 3.0, 99, 106
Wegener, Jonathan, 33–36, 39, 41, 77
West Point, 1
Whalebone, 58, 59
White supremacy/white supremacists, 2, 80
Wikipedia, 1, 2, 5, 6, 11, 17, 19, 21–30, 33, 37, 41, 43, 45, 47, 49, 58, 62, 64, 67, 82, 88, 92, 99, 101, 102, 104–107, 109–111, 115
WikiWikiWeb, 21
Winfrey, Oprah, 44
Wolf, Naomi, 82
World War I, 61, 81
World War II, 23, 27, 57, 61, 62, 66
World Wide Web, 19, 20, 23, 107

Y

Yale, 82, 145
YouTube, 1, 2, 4, 7, 11, 12, 24, 35, 37, 41, 43, 44, 70, 79, 85, 99, 107, 108, 111, 113, 116

Z

Zuckerberg, Mark, 35